Lord, Prepare My Hands for Battle

Prayers Compiled by
Jesse Romero, M.A.

Amor DEUS PUBLISHING

Lord, Prepare My Hands for Battle

(Psalm 144:1 NAB)

Prayers Compiled by
Jesse Romero, M.A.

Cover image: Steven Lopez and Shutterstock.com
Cover and book design: Amor Deus Publishing Design Department

For information regarding permission, write to:
Amor Deus Publishing
Attention: Permissions Dept.
4806 South 40th Street
Phoenix, AZ 85040

ISBN 978-1-61956-514-2

First Edition December 2015
10 9 8 7 6 5 4 3 2 1

Published and printed in the United States of America by Amor Deus Publishing an imprint of Vesuvius Press Incorporated.

Amor DEUS PUBLISHING

Text printed on 30% post-consumer waste recycled paper.

For additional inspirational books visit us at
AmorDeus.com

Dedicated to all priests and lay people doing hand to hand combat with demons in healing – deliverance ministry and praying in front of abortion clinics all around the world. These are the most fearless Catholics in the Church Militant.

Oath of Fidelity

to his Holiness, Pope Francis
in union with the Magisterium
and the Teachings of the One, Holy, Catholic
and Apostolic Church
Founded by Jesus Christ 2000 circa 33A.D.

To Sue

A Message from Jesse Romero

The 3 "C's" of the Christian Warrior are: Conditioning (good works), Concentration (prayer) and Coachability (obedience). This prayer book is designed to vault your faith into the arena of the U.F.C. – *Ultimate Fighting Catholic.* I want you to be part of the M.M.A. – *Mother Mary's Army.* Through prayer and perseverance, we need to feed our FAITH, and DOUBT will starve to death.

This book is my personal prayer workout, designed to make you a Catholic Christian Warrior. It will empower you to become beacons of light in this dark forest of paganism. A person of prayer becomes a burning torch in society to help others navigate safely through the land mines placed by the devil, the world, and the flesh. Battles are never won by being defensive. This book teaches us how to go on the offensive, just like Joshua (chapter 6) in prayer, and bring down the walls of this *'culture of death.'*

This prayer book is not for the faint hearted, it is full contact Catholicism for the serious Soldier of Christ.

—Jesse Romero, M.A.

Jesse Romero

"...for the eyes of the Lord are upon the righteous, and His ears are open to their prayers. But the face of the Lord is against those who do evil..."

—1 Peter 3:12

St. Michael's fight against the dragon…Revelation 12:7

Contents

Section 1: Preparation

Section 3: Engaged in the Battle

Section 4: Catholic Faith Facts

Section 1

Preparation

About Prayer

"For me, prayer is a surge of the heart; it is a simple look turned toward Heaven. It is a cry of recognition and of love, embracing both trial and joy."

—St. Thérèse of Lisieux

"Prayer is conversation with God."

—St. Clement of Alexandria; 3rd century

"Prayer is the best weapon we possess, the key that opens the heart of God."

—St. Padre Pio

"Let my prayer be counted as incense before you."

—Psalm 141:2

"He who practices mental prayer has traveled half the journey. However, he who does not practice at least 15 minutes of mental prayer a day is an animal."

—St. Theresa of Avila

"Those who pray are certainly saved; those who do not pray are certainly damned."

—St. Alphonsus Liguori

Types of Prayer

Bishop Fulton Sheen describes the 3 different types of prayer:[1]

1. *In vocal prayer we go to God on foot.* "Vocal prayer involves praying with particular words, either mentally or out loud. We use our powers of speech to give voice to prayer, wishing to give thanks and praise to God and to ask for the graces necessary to grow in holiness. The Our Father which Jesus taught us to pray is the perfect form of vocal prayer."[2]

2. *In Meditation we go to God on horseback.* "Meditation comes from the Latin word *meditatio*, which means 'thinking over.' A reflective form of prayer, it often begins with reading the Word of God and allowing it to resonate in our mind and heart. Meditation engages our powers of thought and imagination, as well as our emotions and desires. It marshals our interior powers to focus on the mysteries of our faith and on God's will for our lives. The practice of daily meditation is a very important way to grow in holiness."[3]

   St. Isaiah the Hermit (488 AD) sums up for us the grace of meditation: "Meditation melts our evil thoughts and withers the passions of the soul; it enlightens our mind, makes the understanding radiant, and fills the heart with joy. Meditation wounds demons, and drives away thoughts of wickedness. Meditation is a mirror for the mind and light for the conscience; it tames lust, calms fury, dispels wrath, drives away bitterness, and puts irritability to flight. Meditation illuminates the mind and expels laziness. From it is born the tenderness that warms and melts the soul."[4] Living in the presence of God is the key to becoming holy.

There is a study by the name of "the monk study." It showed that certain monks were able to pray and the positive area of the brain, the one that makes us optimistic, it gives us hope, it gives all the neurotransmitters, it improves our immune system, it improves our feeling of wellness, goodbeing and positiveness. It's stimulated by meditation, and they found out that when Americans tried to meditate they weren't able to open up this optimistic center at all, except there was a couple of Americans who could. When they asked what they were meditating they said they were saying the rosary. And so the rosary itself opens up what is called the inferior part of the frontal lobe, there is a thing called the positive optimistic center and the rosary impacted half of that and enhances those feelings of well being, enhances those positive neurotransmitters – dopamine and serotonine which makes us feel healthy, makes us feel active and also prevents Alzheimer's disease.[5]

3. *In Contemplation we go to God in a jet.* "Contemplative prayer is a prayer beyond words, in which we simply gaze upon our Lord in silence and love. It might be likened to the loving silence of a happily married husband and wife who no longer need a lot of words to convey their oneness of mind and heart. Contemplative prayer is a gift of the Holy Spirit that leads us to trustfully surrender ourselves to the Lord and His will for us. The practice of contemplative prayer, as St. Theresa of Avila teaches us, is an indication of our growing friendship with Christ."[6]

St. Thomas Aquinas adds: "contemplation brings us into Gods sweetness, it decreases sadness; it gives us rest from the distraction of the senses, blessing us with the ability to perceive more keenly interior inspirations from God; and it increases, strengthens and directs our affections toward God."[7]

What to Pray For

In St. John's Gospel our Lord Jesus Christ commands us to "ask" in prayer nine times. Supplication and petitionary prayer is God's idea, not just a result of our personal needs. The Lord wants us to ask him for certain things, and Sacred Scripture tells us what the Lord wishes us to pray for.

Self: Pray for personal growth to become Christlike (Colossians 1:9-10) and for personal holiness (1 Thessalonians 4:3). Pray for a deep conviction to evangelize one on one (2 Timothy 2:2).

Family: Pray for your spouse, children, and grandchildren; that your progeny may become an unbroken heritage of God fearing, God loving people.

Community: Pray for the conversion and welfare of your city (Jeremiah 29:7). Pray for a visible witness and unity among God's people in our communities (Philippians 4:2-3).

Church: Pray for the unity of purpose, vision and heart. Pray for the desire to please God rather than people (Philippians 2:1-4).

Church Leaders: Pray for the humility to surrender to the will of God, fidelity to Christ and the Magisterium (Hebrews 13:17; 1 Timothy 5:17).

The Nation: Pray for national repentance (2 Chronicles 7:14), also pray for the moral conscious of our nation to know who God is (Psalms 33:12; Proverbs 14:34).

Leaders In Government: Pray for their wisdom and integrity so that they may be aware of their accountability before the Lord (1 Timothy 2:1-2; Romans 13:1).

Nonbelievers: Pray for their openness to the Holy Spirit's promptings and for their conversion to Christ. Pray that believers will be patient and sensitive with nonbelievers (1 Timothy 2:1-6).

The Sick: Pray for the Lord's healing power of mind, body and soul for someone who is ill (James 5:14-16).

Those In Prison: Pray so that prisoners may come to an understanding of Christ's forgiveness. Pray that the Lord strengthens their resolve against sin and that HE comforts them in their loneliness (Hebrews 13:3; Colossians 4:18).

Children: Pray for the unborn who have been aborted and for those who face abortion today. Pray for those lives that have been devastated by divorce (Malachi 4:6; Matthew 19:14).

A Weekly Prayer Strategy

Sunday: (*Spiritual Growth*) Pray for an outpouring of the gifts of the Holy Spirit so that your faith may be strengthened. That the same Holy Spirit that sanctified those at Pentecost, sanctify our soul with that same transforming fire of God's love.

Monday: (*Family*) Pray for immediate family members and extended family members. Pray also for your friends in Christ so that our Blessed Lord may help us make our home a domestic Church where love reigns.

Tuesday: (*Church & Vocations*) Pray for the Pope, the local Bishop, your Pastor and all your parish clergy. Pray for the marriages and families of all parishioners at your parish, especially those involved in leadership and catechesis. Pray for seminarians, and those who are training and preparing our future priests.

Wednesday: (*Community*) Pray for political leaders in your community. Pray for non-Catholic churches in your area to embrace the fullness of the faith, as well as local Pro-Life efforts, charities, conferences, retreats and other Catholic outreach programs in your diocese.

Thursday: (*Nation*) Pray for the conversion of the President, all federal, state, local elected officials, and military troops.

Friday: (*World*) Pray for world peace and for the missionary efforts of Catholic Missionaries around the world. Pray for the conversion of people who reject the Gospel.

Saturday: (*Afflicted*) Pray for those ministering in dangerous 3rd world countries. Pray for those who are incarcerated, sick and/or hospitalized. Pray for the children of divorce, and those in abusive situations. Pray also for the poor the homeless and the hungry. Pray for families of aborted children.

Catechism of the Catholic Church on Prayer

#2566 – *Man is in search of God.* In the act of creation, God calls every being from nothingness into existence. "Crowned with glory and honor," man is, after the angels, capable of acknowledging "how majestic is the name of the Lord in all the Earth." Even after losing through his sin his likeness to God, man remains an image of his Creator, and retains the desire for the one who calls him into existence. All religions bear witness to men's essential search for God.

#2567 – *God calls man first.* Man may forget his Creator or hide far from his face; he may run after idols or accuse the deity of having abandoned him; yet the living and true God tirelessly calls each person to that mysterious encounter known as prayer. In prayer, the faithful God's initiative of love always comes first; our own first step is always a response. As God gradually reveals himself and reveals man to himself, prayer appears as a reciprocal call, a covenant drama. Through words and actions, this drama engages the heart. It unfolds throughout the whole history of salvation.

Catechism of the Catholic Church on Sacramentals

#1667 – Holy Mother Church has, moreover, instituted sacramentals. These are sacred signs which bear a resemblance to the sacraments. They signify effects, particularly of a spiritual nature, which are obtained through the intercession of the Church. By them men are disposed to receive the chief effect of the sacraments, and various occasions in life are rendered holy.

Characteristics of the Sacramentals

#1668 – Sacramentals are instituted for the sanctification of certain ministries of the Church, certain states of life, a great variety of circumstances in Christian life, and the use of many things helpful to man. In accordance with bishops' pastoral decisions, they can also respond to the needs, culture, and special history of the Christian people of a particular region or time. They always include a prayer, often accompanied by a specific sign, such as the laying on of hands, the sign of the cross, or the sprinkling of holy water (which recalls Baptism).

#1669 – Sacramentals derive from the baptismal priesthood: every baptized person is called to be a "blessing," and to bless. Hence lay people may preside at certain blessings; the more a blessing concerns ecclesial and sacramental life, the more is its administration reserved to the ordained ministry (bishops, priests, or deacons).

"A father's blessing gives a person firm roots..."

—Sirach 3:9

#1670 – Sacramentals do not confer the grace of the Holy Spirit in the way that the sacraments do, but by the Church's prayer, they prepare us to receive grace and dispose us to cooperate with it. "For well-disposed members of the faithful, the liturgy of the sacraments and sacramentals sanctifies almost every event of their lives with the divine grace which flows from the Paschal mystery of the Passion, Death, and Resurrection of Christ. From this source all sacraments and sacramentals draw their power. There is scarcely any proper use of material things which cannot be thus directed toward the sanctification of men and the praise of God."

Various forms of Sacramentals

Exorcism

#1673 – When the Church asks publicly and authoritatively in the name of Jesus Christ that a person or object be protected against the power of the Evil One and withdrawn from his dominion, it is called exorcism. Jesus performed exorcisms and from him the Church has received the power and office of exorcizing. In a simple form, exorcism is performed at the celebration of Baptism. The solemn exorcism, called "a major exorcism," can be performed only by a priest and with the permission of the bishop. The priest must proceed with prudence, strictly observing the rules established by the Church. Exorcism is directed at the expulsion of demons or to the liberation from demonic possession through the spiritual authority which Jesus entrusted to his Church. Illness, especially psychological illness, is a very different matter; treating this is the concern of medical science. Therefore, before an exorcism is performed, it is important to ascertain that one is dealing with the presence of the Evil One, and not an illness.

A Catholic Priest can do a minor exorcism (aka – deliverance ministry) of his own accord without permission from his bishop. There is an actual book known as the "manual of minor exorcisms"[8] that ever Priest should have in his "tool box."

Popular Piety

#1674 – Besides sacramental liturgy and sacramentals, catechesis must take into account the forms of piety and popular devotions among the faithful. The religious sense of the Christian people has always found expression in various forms of piety surrounding the Church's sacramental life, such as the veneration of relics, visits to sanctuaries, pilgrimages, processions, the Stations of the Cross, religious dances, the rosary, medals, etc.

#1675 – These expressions of piety extend the liturgical life of the Church, but do not replace it. They "should be so drawn up that they harmonize with the liturgical seasons, accord with the sacred liturgy, are in some way derived from it and lead the people to it, since in fact the liturgy by its very nature is far superior to any of them."

Common Sacramentals

Holy Water

Holy Water is a sacramental that remits venial sin. Because of the blessing attached to it, Holy Mother Church strongly urges its use upon her children, especially when dangers threaten, such as fire, storms, sickness and other calamities. Every Catholic home should have a supply of holy water. Most Catholics do not take sufficient advantage of the benefits derived from holy water. Untold spiritual wealth is concentrated in a tiny drop of blessed water. If we would realize now, as we shall realize after death, the many benefits which may be derived from holy water, we would use it far more frequently and with greater faith and reverence. Holy

Water has its great power and efficacy from the prayers of the Church, which its Divine Founder always accepts with complacency.

The Priest prays to God When He Blesses Water: *"O God,...grant that this creature of Thine (water) may be endowed with divine grace to drive away devils and to cast out diseases, that whatever in the houses or possessions of the faithful may be sprinkled by this water, may be freed from everything unclean, and delivered from what is hurtful...Let everything that threatens the safety or peace of the dwellers therein be banished by the sprinkling of this water; so that the health which they seek by calling upon Thy Holy Name may be guarded from all assault."*

Prayer over oneself with Holy Water: *"By this Holy Water and by Thy Precious Blood, cleanse me from my sins, O Lord" or "By this Holy Water and by the Precious Blood, wash away all my sins, O Lord — Amen."*

The devil hates holy water because of its power over him. He cannot long abide in a place or near a person that is often sprinkled with this blessed water. If your dear ones live at a distance, holy water, sprinkled with faith and piety, can move the Sacred Heart to bless your loved ones and protect them from all harm of soul and body. When worry and fear take possession of your heart, hasten to your holy water font, and give your dear ones the benefit of the Church's prayers. The holy souls long for it. Only in Purgatory can one understand how ardently a poor soul longs for holy water. The holy souls nearest to Heaven may need the sprinkling of only one drop to relieve their souls. Holy water was first used in the Old Testament.

> *"...and the priest shall take holy water in an earthen vessel, and take some of the dust that is on the floor of the tabernacle and put it into the water."*
>
> —Numbers 5:17

"And Eli'sha sent a messenger to him, saying, 'Go and wash in the Jordan seven times, and your flesh shall be restored, and you shall be clean.' But Na'aman was angry, and went away, saying, 'Behold, I thought that he would surely come out to me, and stand, and call on the name of the LORD his God, and wave his hand over the place, and cure the leper. Are not Aba'na and Pharpar, the rivers of Damascus, better than all the waters of Israel? Could I not wash in them, and be clean?' So he turned and went away in a rage. But his servants came near and said to him, 'My father, if the prophet had commanded you to do some great thing, would you not have done it? How much rather, then, when he says to you, `Wash, and be clean'?' So he went down and dipped himself seven times in the Jordan, according to the word of the man of God; and his flesh was restored like the flesh of a little child, and he was clean."

—2 Kings 5:10-14

Blessed Salt

Blessed salt is an instrument of grace to preserve one from the corruption of evil occurring from sin, sickness, demonic influence, etc. As in the case of all sacramentals, its power comes not from the sign itself, but by means of the Church's official liturgical prayer of blessing, a power the Church derives from Christ Himself. (Matthew 16:19 and 18:18). As the Vatican II document on the Sacred Liturgy states (paragraph 60-61), *that both Sacraments and sacramentals sanctify us, not of themselves, but by power flowing from the redemptive act of Jesus, elicited by the Church's intercession to be directed through those external signs and elements.* Hence sacramentals like blessed salt, holy water, medals, etc., are not to be used superstitiously as having self-contained power, but as 'focus points' funneling one's faith toward Jesus, just as handkerchiefs were used to focus faith for healing and deliverance (Acts 19:12). Thus, used non-superstitiously, modest amounts of blessed salt may be sprinkled in one's bedroom, or across thresholds to prevent burglary, in cars for safety, etc. A few grains of blessed salt in drinking water or used in cooking or as food seasoning often bring astonishing spiritual and physical benefits.

As with the use of Sacraments, much depends on the faith and devotion of the person using the blessed salt or any sacramental. This faith must be centered in Jesus Christ. Any amount of salt may be presented to a priest for his blessing using the following official prayer from the Roman Ritual:

> *"Almighty God, we ask you to bless this salt, as once you blessed the salt scattered over the water by the prophet Elisha. Wherever this salt (and water) is sprinkled, drive away the power of evil, and protect us always by the presence of your Holy Spirit. Grant this through Christ our Lord — Amen."*

If you are interested in getting blessed salt, print this information out and present the blessing prayer to your parish priest. Ask him to bless the salt using the official prayer from the Roman Ritual above.[9]

The Miraculous Medal

St. Maximilian said "the Miraculous Medal" is a "spiritual bullet" in the war to win souls. He called the Miraculous Medal "a 'bullet' with which the faithful soldier hits the enemy that is evil, and thus rescues souls." The medal was given to us by Our Lady of Rue du Bac in 1830. The front proclaims Mary as Immaculate Conception and Mediatrix of All Graces; the back side as Coredemptrix.

The Miraculous Medal owes its origins to the apparitions of the Blessed Virgin Mary in the chapel of the Rue du Bac, Paris, in 1830. She appeared to Catherine Labouré, showing the young nun and future saint the design of a medal that serves as a mini-catechism of the Church's teaching on Our Lady.

In a vision, Mary stood on a globe with brilliant light streaming from her jeweled fingers. "Behold the symbol of graces shed upon those who ask for them," she said, representing herself as Mediatrix of All Graces. Surrounding her was a banner which read, "O Mary, conceived without sin, pray for us who have recourse to thee," symbolizing her Immaculate Conception. The vision reversed, showing the letter 'M' entwined with a cross above the Sacred Hearts. This image represents Mary as Coredemptrix, a unique participator in Jesus' saving act of redemption.

Millions of medals have been distributed and untold graces given "to those who wear it around the neck" as the Virgin promised to St. Catherine. Hearing of the miraculous conversion of the agnostic Alphonse Ratisbonne through the miraculous medal, St. Maximilian made wearing it and giving it away an integral part of his movement.

For Consecration to Our Lady, and how to perform it:
www.consecration.com.

The Brown Scapular of Our Lady of Mount Carmel

One of the signs in the tradition of the Church from many centuries ago is the Brown Scapular of Our Lady of Mount Carmel. It is a spiritual sign approved by the Church and accepted by the Carmelite Order as an external sign of love for Mary, of the trust her children have in her, and of a commitment to live like her.

The Scapular finds its roots in the tradition of the Order, which has seen in it a sign of Mary's Motherly protection. It stands for a commitment to follow Jesus, like Mary, the perfect model of all the Disciples of Christ. This commitment finds its origin in baptism by which we become children of God. It is an expression of our belief that we will meet God in eternal life, aided by the intercession and prayers of Mary.

The Scapular aids us to live authentic Christian lives in line with the Gospel. It helps us to frequent the sacraments, to profess our special devotion to the Blessed Virgin, which should be expressed each day, at least by saying the Hail Mary three times a day.

> *Hail Mary, full of grace, the Lord is with Thee. Blessed art Thou among women and Blessed is the fruit of Thy womb, Jesus. Holy Mary, Mother of God pray for us sinners, now and at the hour of our death — Amen.*[10]

The Saint Benedict Medal

Origin of the Medal of Saint Benedict: For the early Christians, the cross was a favorite symbol and badge of their faith in Christ. From the writings of St. Gregory the Great (540-604), we know that St. Benedict had a deep faith in the Cross and worked miracles with the sign of the cross. This faith in, and special devotion to the Cross was passed on to succeeding generations of Benedictines.

Devotion to the Cross of Christ also gave rise to the striking of medals that bore the image of St. Benedict holding a cross aloft in his right hand and his Rule for Monasteries in the other hand. Thus, the Cross has always been closely associated with the Medal of St. Benedict, which is often referred to as the Medal-Cross of St. Benedict. In the course of time, other additions were made, such as the Latin petition on the margin of the medal, asking that by St. Benedict's presence we may be strengthened in the hour of death, as will be explained later.

We do not know just when the first medal of St. Benedict was struck. At some point in history a series of capital letters was placed around the large figure of the cross on the reverse side of the medal. For a long time the meaning of these letters was unknown, but in 1647 a manuscript dating back to 1415 was found at the Abbey of Metten in Bavaria, giving an explanation of the letters. They are the initial letters of a Latin prayer of exorcism against Satan.

The medal is a prayer of exorcism against Satan, a prayer for strength in time of temptation, a prayer for peace among ourselves and among the nations of the world, a prayer that the Cross of Christ be our light and guide, a prayer of firm rejection of all that is evil, a prayer of petition that we may with Christian courage "walk in God's ways, with the Gospel as our guide," as St. Benedict urges us.

A profitable spiritual experience can be ours if we but take the time to study the array of inscriptions and representations found on the two sides of the medal. The lessons found there can be pondered over and over to bring true peace of mind and heart into our lives as we struggle to overcome the weaknesses of our human nature and realize that our human condition is not perfect, but that with the help of God and the intercession of St. Benedict and all the saints, our condition can become better.

The Medal of St. Benedict can serve as a constant reminder of the need for us to take up our cross daily and "follow the true King, Christ our Lord," and thus learn "to share in his heavenly kingdom," as St. Benedict urges us in the Prologue of his Rule.

The Cross of Eternal Salvation: On the face of the medal is the image of Saint Benedict. In his right hand he holds the cross, the Christian's symbol of salvation. The cross reminds us of the zealous work of evangelizing and civilizing England and Europe carried out mainly by the Benedictine monks and nuns, especially from the sixth to the tenth centuries.

Rule and Raven: In St. Benedict's left hand is his Rule for Monasteries that could well be summed up in the words of the Prologue exhorting us to "walk in God's ways, with the Gospel as our guide." On a pedestal to the right of St. Benedict is the poisoned cup that was intended to kill him, the poisoned cup shattered when he made the sign of the cross over it. On a pedestal to the left is a raven about to carry away a loaf of poisoned bread that a jealous enemy had sent to St. Benedict.

C. S. P. B.: Above the cup and the raven are the Latin words: *Crux sancti. Patris Benedicti* (The Cross of our holy father Benedict). On the margin of the medal, encircling the figure of Benedict, are the Latin words: *Ejus in obitu nostro praesentia muniamur!* (May we be strengthened by his presence in the hour of our death!). Benedictines have always regarded St. Benedict as a special patron of a happy death. He himself died in the chapel at Montecassino while standing with his arms raised up to Heaven, supported by the brothers of the monastery. St. Benedict died shortly after he received Holy Communion.

Cross Beams: On the back of the medal, the cross is dominant. On the vertical and horizontal beams of the cross are the initial letters of a rhythmic Latin prayer: *Crux sancta sit mihi lux! Non draco sit mihi dux!* (May the holy cross be my light! May the dragon never be my guide!). In the quadrants of the cross, the letters "C S P B" stand for *Crux Sancti Patris Benedicti* (The cross of our holy father Benedict).

Pax: Above the cross is the word *"PAX"* (peace) that has been a Benedictine motto for centuries. Around the margin of the back of the medal, the letters "V R S N S M V - S M Q L I V B" are the initial letters, as mentioned above, of a Latin prayer of exorcism against Satan: *"Vade retro Satana! Nunquam suade mihi vana! Sunt mala quae libas. Ipse venena bibas!"* (Begone Satan! Never tempt me with your vanities! What you offer me is evil. Drink the poison yourself!)

Use of the Medal: There is no special way prescribed for carrying or wearing the Medal of St. Benedict. It can be worn on a chain around the neck, attached to one's rosary, kept in one's pocket or purse, or placed in one's car or in one's place of business. The purpose of using the medal in any of the above ways is to call down God's blessing and protection upon us, wherever we are, and upon our homes and possessions, especially through the intercession of St. Benedict. By the conscious and devout use of the medal, it becomes, as it were, a constant silent prayer and reminder to us of our dignity as followers of Christ.

The use of any religious article is intended as a means of reminding us of God and of stirring up in us a ready willingness and desire to serve God and our neighbor. With this understanding we reject any use of religious articles as if they were mere charms or had some magic power to bring us good luck or better health. Such is not the Christian attitude.

It is recommended that everyone wear the Medal or Crucifix of St. Benedict as a powerful defense in the spiritual war that we are battling every day. By doing so we call for the intercession of St. Benedict, who is a powerful ally in spiritual warfare. The St. Benedict Medal is the only medal in the church that has an exorcism prayer placed on it.[11]

The Sign of the Cross

Some things become so familiar that we take them for granted. A good practice would be to stop and think about what we're doing when we make the Sign of the Cross. The Cross is the center of Christianity; it signifies the deepest surrender to God's will. As we recall at the Baptismal ceremony, "We die with Christ to rise again in Him." When I make the sign of the Cross, I affirm my own surrender to God's will. While tracing the sign over my body, I pray that

I will live as a member of God's kingdom.

CCC #1235 – *The sign of the cross,* on the threshold of the celebration, marks with the imprint of Christ the one who is going to belong to him and signifies the grace of the redemption Christ won for us by his cross.

1. Father, Son and Holy Spirit (3 fingers).

2. One God (bring fingers together – index finger and thumb).

3. Jesus came down to Earth to save us (from head to stomach). Roman Guardini (1885-1968), the great theologian prior to Vatican II stated: "Cross yourself from head to stomach, from shoulder to shoulder."

4. God saved us through the cross and transferred us from left to right (Matthew 25:33). The left signifies 'damnation' the right signifies 'mercy.' Pope Innocent III (13th century) said: "Make the sign of the cross from left to right, which means from death to life, from misery to glory." Ecclesiastes 10:2 "A wise man's heart inclines him toward the right, but a fool's heart toward the left."

5. We love God with all our mind, heart, soul and strength. We touch our head, heart, left shoulder and right shoulder – which is a physical demonstration of the first and greatest commandment.

6. We belong to the Lord Jesus Christ and are sealed with the sign of the cross and nothing will ever separate us from his love (we're sacramentally branded).

7. We worship God with our mind, heart and body out of gratitude because the precious blood of His Son Jesus Christ, was shed on the cross for my sins.

8. Holy water is a reminder that we are under oath; it reminds us of our baptismal promises and our participation as citizens of Heaven in the household of God (cf. Ephesians 2:19).

Why do we make the sign of the Cross? Probably no action identifies a person as a Catholic Christian so easily as the Sign of the Cross. From the earliest times of the Church, this sign of the cross was used in all the Sacraments, and as a means of recognizing other Christians in time of persecution. In the earliest times of the Church, the sign of the cross was drawn by the thumb on the forehead, in much the same way as Catholics *cross* themselves on the forehead, lips and breast, before the reading of the Gospel at Holy Mass.

- The Christian writer Tertullian (160 A.D.- 225 A.D.) wrote for Fathers to teach sons: "In all our travels, in our coming in and going out, in putting on our clothes and our shoes, at table, in going to rest, whatever we are doing we mark our forehead with the sign of the cross."

- Saint Ephrem the Syrian (306 A.D. - 373 A.D.) wrote: "My son, mark all you do with the sign of the life giving cross. Do not go out from the door of your house until you have signed yourself with the sign of the cross. Do not neglect to make that sign whether you are eating or drinking, or going to sleep, whether you are at home, or going on a journey. There is no habit to be compared with it. Let it be like a wall that protects you and your conduct; teach it to your children so that they may faithfully learn the custom."

- Saint Augustine of Hippo in the 4th century (Sermon on Psalm 141) said: "Let me not have my forehead bare – let the cross of my Lord cover it."

- Lactantius, a Christian advisor to Emperor Constantine – "Diocletian…during his abode in the East he began to slay victims…while he sacrificed, some attendants of his, who were Christians, stood by, and they put *the immortal sign* on their foreheads. At this the *demons* were chased away, and the holy rites interrupted…"

- Ezekiel 9: 4 "'Go through the city, through Jerusalem, and put a mark upon the foreheads of the men who sign and groan over all the abominations that are committed in it.' And to the others he said in my hearing, 'Pass through the city after him, and smite; your eyes shall not spare, and you shall show no pity; slay old men outright, young men and maidens, little children and woman, but touch no one upon whom is the mark.'" *Judgment always begins in the house of God* (1 Peter 4:17) and those Israelites in the days of Ezekiel who were engaged in idolatry and abused the holy things of God incurred His judgment. The Israelites that were spared were those that did not worship false gods, they were sealed with the Hebrew letter 'Tau' which is the form of a cross. This sign (*the cross*) on their forehead was the mark that singled out the Israelites who were to be spared from the destruction of Jerusalem the first time it was destroyed in 587 B.C. In Revelation 7:3 and 14:1, John the Evangelist alludes to those servants of God in the "New Jerusalem" as being marked with the sign of the cross that Ezekiel spoke about (cf. chapter 9:4-6).

Just like the Jews do not want the world to forget about the Holocaust so they make movies, make documentaries, have museums and they give tours to the Holocaust locations. We as Catholic Christians do not want the world to forget the incredible Passion of Christ and His death on a cross. This is what it cost Him to redeem the world and make atonement for our sins. Jesus Christ paid a debt that he did not owe, because we owe a debt that we cannot pay.

Quotes to Ponder

A perceptive observer of our time spoke a sobering truth for America:

> *"The self-sufficient do not pray, the self-satisfied will not pray, the self-righteous cannot pray."*
>
> — Unknown

> *"Prayer is the oxygen of the soul."*
>
> — Saint Padre Pio

> *"Pray as if everything depends on God and act as if everything depends on you."*
>
> — Saint Augustine

> *"Work as if you were to live 100 years. Pray as if you were to die tomorrow."*
>
> — Benjamin Franklin

> *"He who prays is saved. He who prays not is damned."*
>
> —St. Alphonsus Liguori

> *"He who practices mental prayer has traveled half the journey. However, he who does not practice at least 15 minutes of mental prayer a day is an animal"*
>
> —St. Teresa of Avila.

PUSH = Pray, Until, Something, Happens.

PRAY = Praise, Reflect, Ask, Yearn.

Pray daily and pray often, we can only stand tall against evil, as long as we stay on our knees before our Lord.

A State of Grace

"Living in a State of Grace, basically means imitating Jesus Christ and cultivating an interior life. The only possible way to live in a state of grace is 'through Him, with Him and in Him.'"

—Jesse Romero

There are some very basic rules that all Catholics should know, but some are either ignorant of them, or knowingly fail to follow them. The following three Bible verses will give us guiding principles in order to live in "a state of grace."

"...be an imitator *of me as I (Paul) am of Christ."*

—1 Corinthians 11:1

"...imitate *me (Paul) as I imitate the Lord..."*

—1 Thessalonians 1:6-7

"...so be imitators *of God, as beloved children, and live in love..."*

—Ephesians 5:1

In addition to these verses of scripture, one of the best-selling books in Catholicism is authored by a monk, Thomas A. Kempis (14th century), entitled, *The Imitation of Christ*. We come to the very obvious conclusion that the best strategy to live the Christian life is: 'Imitate Jesus'! That's the key! We must admit that the Catholic Church is too good to be true, and yet, too hard to be followed and lived perfectly – only but for the 'grace' of Almighty God. Let us remember the timeless words of Saint Augustine, "If you pray well you will live well, if you live well you will die well; and if you die well all will be well."

Here are some ancient and recent words from those who know the power of living in "a state of grace."

> *"...a soul in the state of grace has nothing to fear from demons, who are cowards capable of running away from the look of a child..."*
>
> —St. Thérèse of Liseux
> (Doctor of the Church,
> from *The Story of a Soul,* Chapter 1)

> *"...1st state of protection against demons – live in a state of grace..."*
>
> —Fr. Chad Ripperger F.S.S.P. – Exorcist

> *"...the best shield and armor against the attacks of the Evil One is prayer, the Sacraments, good works and living a spiritual life."*
>
> —Fr Antonio Fortea – Exorcist[12]

> *"Certainly, a person who prays and lives in God's grace will be protected by God."*
>
> —Fr Antonio Fortea – Exorcist, Spain[13]

> "Just as the demon fights against us daily, so we must battle against him. Through the strength of the Spirit that was given to us, we are certain of the victory. To live in a state of grace means always to say Yes to Christ and No to Satan, according to our baptismal promises: if we do not, we fall into

sin…Safeguarding and increasing the state of grace is a victory against ordinary activity of the demon (temptation), and, at the same time, it is the best prevention against his extraordinary activity… Again, we must remember that the best means of prevention is to abide in the grace of God, pray, receive the sacraments, and ask for the intercession of the Virgin Mary, the angels and the saints."[14]

"…A state of grace is the spiritual condition of an individual who has sanctifying grace in his soul. That is, he is free from mortal sin and seriously disordered inclinations to sin. Any 'state' can be lost (i.e., a state of mind, a state of euphoria, a state of favor with another person), and the state of grace can be lost simply by the commission of one mortal sin. Venial sin denigrates and weakens the state of grace but does not destroy it in the soul. It cannot be said enough that the 'state of grace', and the attempt to live an authentic life of faith, are the greatest protections from evil for everyone, even those not of our faith." [15]

The practice of RADICAL Catholicism is required to break demonic influence. To live in a 'state of grace', will be required of you for the rest of your life. *Radical* comes from the Latin word 'radix' which means to be "rooted."[16] Jesus doesn't need fans, he needs followers, He doesn't need spectators, he needs gladiators.

Living in a State of Grace

"There are 50 states in our country. There is 1 state every Catholic should want to live in, thats 'the state of grace.' There is 1 state nobody should want to live in, thats in 'the state of mortal sin.'"

—Jesse Romero

The following twelve points are given to the reader with the intention of providing 'Spiritual Direction.' These points explain from Scripture and the wisdom of Mother Church, how to resist the devil. This type of spiritual training is not for the faint hearted, but will definitely teach and help you to "Live in a State of Grace"[17] and thus be a disciple of Christ.

1. Your Philosophy of Life must be the following: "God put us in the world to know, to love, and to serve him, and so to come to paradise." (CCC #1721). This is what the Holy Bible means when it says "...take every thought captive to obey Christ" (2 Corinthians 10:5) or "But we have the mind of Christ" (1 Corinthians 2:16) or "Do not be conformed to this world but be transformed by the renewal of your mind, that you may prove what is the will of God, what is good and acceptable and perfect" (Romans 12:2). This means we were made to have a relationship with God.

   "...man, himself created in the 'image of God' and called to a personal relationship with God..."

   —CCC #299

   "...requires that the faithful believe in it, and that they celebrate it, and that they live from it in a vital and personal relationship with the living and true God. This relationship is prayer."

   —CCC #2558

2. Every Catholic must form their moral conscience in order to know what is "right" and what is "wrong." At the very least, one must know the 10 Commandments (Exodus 20:1-17 and Deuteronomy 5:6-21), 7 Capital Sins (Proverbs 6:16-19), the 7 Virtues (Wisdom 8:7, 1 Corinthians 13:13, CCC #1834, CCC #1841) and the 5 precepts of the Church (cf. CCC #2042-2043). An important part of living

in a state of grace, is examining your conscience each night before you go to bed (cf. Lamentations 3:40; 1 Corinthians 11:28, 2 Corinthians 13:5). This helps form our moral conscience according to the Word of God (CCC #1776-1802). Forming our moral conscience gives us 'moral clarity' and the ability to know right from wrong, black and white, good and evil, darkness and light, decent and indecent. Proverbs 3:5-7, "Trust in the Lord with all your heart, and do not rely on your own insight. In all your ways acknowledge him, and he will make straight your paths. Be not wise in your own eyes; fear the Lord, and turn away from evil."

3. Regular confession is a healthy spiritual practice, it is recommended we go to Confession at least once a month.[18] In todays corrosive culture of death, monthly confession is almost the minimum required for someone who is serious about spiritual progress. I suggest you try to go to the same priest if possible so he can get to know you. Would you go to a different dentist every 4 months? Hmm. A Catholic is required to go to Confession at least once a year (CCC#1457). The effects of Confession according to the Catechism (CCC#1468) are spiritual consolation, peace and serenity of conscience, this is the opposite of Hell (which is perpetual remorse of conscience). If one is guilty of mortal sin, go to Confession as soon as possible. For a sin to be mortal, 3 conditions must be present: "Mortal sin is sin whose object is grave matter, and which is also committed with full knowledge and deliberate consent" (CCC #1857). The Catechism and the Holy Bible make a distinction between mortal and venial sins (CCC #1857,1863, 1 John 5:16-17). Confession is the Sacrament of Humility. The 3 degrees of humility are Meekness, Mortification, and Detachment. Fr Antonio Fortea

(Spain – Exorcist) says:

"...confession is a divine gift much greater than exorcism. Exorcism only drives out a demon from one's body; confession drives out evil from our souls...Frequent confession strengthens us in sanctifying grace and is a powerful force in helping us resist to temptation."[19]

Fr Gabriel Amorth (Vatican Exorcist) says:

[Confession] "is the most direct means to fight Satan, because it is the sacrament that tears souls from the demons grasp, strengthens against sin, unites us more closely to God, and helps to conform our souls increasingly to the divine will. I advise frequent confession, possibly weekly, to all victims of evil activities."[20]

It is very very rare that a person who is in a state of grace can become possessed, however, it could occur only through divine permission by God.[21]

4. Attend Holy Mass each Sunday and Holy Days of Obligation (CCC #2180 - 2181). Attend daily Mass when possible, the more sanctifying grace you receive the better.

"The world could exist more easily without the sun than without the Mass."

—St. Padre Pio

"All the good works in the world are not equal to the Holy Sacrifice of the Mass because they are the works of men; but the Mass is the work of God. Martyrdom is nothing in comparison, for it is but the sacrifice of man to God; but the Mass is the sacrifice of God for man."

—St. John Marie Vianney (1786-1859)

"The celebration of the Holy Mass is as valuable as the death of Jesus on the Cross."

—St. Thomas Aquinas

"Man should tremble, the world should vibrate, all Heaven should be deeply moved when the Son of God appears on the altar in the hands of the Priest."

—St. Francis of Assisi

5. Visit the Blessed Sacrament (Adoration) at least once a week and pray a rosary, divine mercy chaplet, read your Bible, your Catechism or some other good spiritual book. St. Thomas Aquinas, St. Jose Maria de Escriva and St. John Henry Newman wrote some of the most beautiful prayers on there knees before the Blessed Sacrament.[22] Many saints did a daily Holy Hour in Eucharistic Adoration in silent contemplation (like St. John Vianney – the cure of Ars). Believe with all your heart in the True Presence, Body, Blood, Soul, and Divinity, of Our Lord and Savior Jesus Christ in the Holy Eucharist and ask Him to save, sanctify and set you free.

   "...By the consecration the transubstantiation of the bread and wine into the Body and Blood of Christ is brought about. Under the consecrated species of bread and wine, Christ himself, living and glorious, is present in a true, real, and substantial manner: his Body and his Blood, with his soul and his divinity."

   —CCC #1413

   "Because Christ himself is present in the sacrament of the altar, He is to be honored with

> *the worship of adoration. 'To visit the Blessed Sacrament is…a proof of gratitude, an expression of love, and a duty of adoration toward Christ our Lord.'"*
>
> —CCC #1418

6. Pray the Most Holy Rosary daily. Fr Patrick Peyton, who started a ministry called *The Family Rosary Crusade,* wrote in 1947 that "the Family that prays together stays together" and "a World at prayer is a World at Peace." Fr. Peyton proclaimed this call to prayer tirelessly throughout the media.

"…pray constantly…"

—1 Thessalonians 5:17

"Give me an army saying the rosary and I will conquer the world."

—Pope Pius IX

Praying the Rosary is a spiritual powerhouse of prayer because you are saying the two names that the devil most fears – "JESUS and MARY" 50 times. It is like having a spiritual 50 caliber machine gun that makes the devil and Hell tremble as the words roll off of our tongues with faith, hope and love. The Rosary will give you and your children the power we need to reject the temptations of the evil one, power to reject the false teachings of this world and to reject the allure of the Culture of Death and in so doing you preserve yourselves strong as Temples of the Holy Spirit. Put on the Armor of God and stand Firm on the solid foundation of the Catholic Faith. A 24-hour day has 1,440 minutes. Can't you give 1% of 1,440 minutes each day to God? If so, pray the daily rosary in 15 minutes = 1% of a 24 hour day.

7. Pray the Divine Mercy daily at 3pm if possible, on your knees with rosary beads. Jesus died at 3pm, therefore, it is known as the "hour of Mercy." Here are some of the promises made by Our Lord Jesus Christ to St. Faustina:

   "Whoever will recite it will receive great mercy at the hour of death."

   —*Diary*, 687

   "When they say this chaplet in the presence of the dying, I will stand between My Father and the dying person, not as the just Judge but as the Merciful Savior."

   —*Diary*, 1541

   "Priests will recommend it to sinners as their last hope of salvation. Even if there were a sinner most hardened, if he were to recite this chaplet only once, he would receive grace from My infinite mercy."

   —*Diary*, 687

   "I desire to grant unimaginable graces to those souls who trust in My mercy."

   —*Diary*, 687

   "Through the Chaplet you will obtain everything, if what you ask for is compatible with My will."

   —*Diary*, 1731

8. Pray the Angelus at 12 noon daily. Pope St. Pius V (and countless other saints), prayed the Angelus 3 times a day (6am, 12noon, 6pm), in addition to the holy rosary. The Pope St. Pius V said this prayer along with the holy rosary were instrumental in defeating the Muslim Turk invaders at the Sea Battle of Lepanto in 1571.

   A short Catechesis on prayer tells us:

i. "Pray without ceasing" (1 Thessalonians 5:17). That admonition clearly indicates that prayer is to be, at every moment, a part of our lives. Jesus also prayed for us in John chapter 17:20-21 and in Matthew chapter 6:5-8.

ii. Jesus gave us a model prayer and in Matthew 26:41, he pleaded with Peter, James and John to pray so that, "...you may not undergo the test. The spirit is willing, but the flesh is weak."

iii. We should be praying at least 3 times a day according to Daniel 6:10-11.

9. First of all end your night by thanking God for the gift of life and the gift of eternal life. Than, make an "Examination of Conscience" before bedtime and then pray an "Act of Contrition." In other words, look at your day and honestly ask your self introspectively what virtues (moral excellence, good habits) did I live out today, what did I do that pleased God. Ask yourself what vice (wrong, sins) did I commit today, what did I do that offended God. We must confess our "venial" sins to the Lord daily (CCC #1458). If you pray the "Act of Contrition" each night and or bless yourself with holy water with a contrite heart before going to bed, your venial sins are remitted (cf. pages 75 to 76 'Prayers of Repentance'). Gods mercy is like a windshield wiper, we keep on sinning and He keeps on wiping IF, we repent, confess and amend our sinful ways. These 3 things: repent, confess and amend our sinful ways turn on Gods windshield wipers.

God WANTS to forgive your sins. Here is what he says: "Come now, let us set things right, says the Lord: though your sins be like scarlet, they may become white as snow; though they be red like crimson, they may become white as wool" (Isaiah 1:18 NAB).

- Bad news: nature doesn't forgive and doesn't forget.
- Bad news: man forgives but doesn't forget.
- Good news: God forgives and forgets.

"...says the Lord; for I will forgive their iniquity, and I will remember their sin no more."

—Jeremiah 31:34

"I am He who blots out your transgressions for my own sake, and I will not remember your sins."

—Isaiah 43:25

10. Read the Holy Bible daily with the heart of the Church by following the daily Mass readings. The Church grants a plenary indulgence to those who read the Bible for 30 minutes a day (provided all the conditions for an indulgence are met). "A partial indulgence is granted to the faithful who use Sacred Scripture for spiritual reading with the veneration due the word of God. A plenary indulgence is granted if the reading continues for at least one half hour."[23]

    St. Jerome said, "Ignorance of the Scripture is ignorance of Christ."

    St. Teresa of Avila, stated, "All the troubles of the Church, all the evils in the world flow from this source; that men do not by clear and sound knowledge and serious consideration, penetrate into the truths of Sacred Scripture."

St. Augustine reminds us that, "When we pray, we speak to God. When we read Scripture, God speaks to us."

God did not design the Bible to be a dark puzzle for bright scholars, but to be a bright lamp for travelers through a dark world. When you carry the Bible, Satan gets a headache. When you open it, he collapses. When he sees you reading it, he faints! In order to fight 'truth decay,' we need to read our Bible.

B asic
I nstruction
B efore
L eaving
E arth

11. Read the *Catechism of the Catholic Church*, a few chapters a day if possible, it takes about 5 minutes or some other spiritual reading (discipline yourself). Knowledge is power. The worst thing to be is a "low information Catholic."

"Carefully study to present thyself approved unto God, a workman that needeth not to be ashamed, rightly handling the word of truth."

—2 Timothy 2:15 (Douay Rheims Bible)

12. Listen to Catholic radio and/or television throughout the day. Feed yourself spiritually. Listen to Catholic (Christian) music especially in the evening when preparing for bed. Include especially, Gregorian chant. Praising God and sacred music expels evil spirits and fills the environment with the holy presence of God (cf. 1 Samuel 16:14-23; Acts 16:25-26). It brings in the sweet aroma of Christ (cf. 2

Corinthians 2:15) to your home. Sacred music encourages us to be holy (cf. Ephesians 5:19). Music is so powerful that the angels sing to God in Heaven day and night forever and ever (cf. Revelation 4:8-11; Isaiah 6:1-4). Sacred Scripture tells us that God inhabits the praises of His people – "Yet thou art holy, enthroned on the praises of Israel" (Psalm 22:3 R.S.V.). A believer who praises and worships the Lord in song without shame, is the voice of a soul set free from sin. Finally, remember that St Augustine says: "He who sings prays twice."

Examination of Conscience and Confession

Examination of Conscience

Did I deny or doubt God's existence?

Did I refuse to believe God's revelation?

Did I believe in horoscopes, fortune telling, dreams, good luck charms or reincarnation?

Did I deny that I was a Catholic?

Did I abandon the Catholic Faith?

Did I despair of or presume on God's mercy?

Did I neglect prayer for a long time?

Did I fail to pray daily?

Did I blaspheme God or take God's Name in vain, curse or break an oath or vow?

Did I miss Mass on a Sunday or on a Holy Day of Obligation through my own fault?

Am I always reverent in the presence of the Most Blessed Sacrament?

Was I inattentive at Mass?

Did I arrive at Mass late?

Did I leave Mass early?

Did I do unnecessary servile work on Sunday?

Did I disobey or disrespect my parents or legitimate superiors?

Did I neglect my duties to my husband, wife, children or parents?

Did I fail to actively take an interest in the religious education and formation of my children?

Have I failed to educate myself concerning the teachings of the Church?

Did I give a full day's work in return for a full day's pay?

Did I give scandal by what I said or did, especially to the young?

Was I the cause of anyone abandoning the Catholic Faith?

Did I give a fair wage to my employee(s)?

Was I impatient, angry, envious, unkind, proud, jealous, revengeful, hateful toward others or lazy?

Did I give bad example, abuse drugs, drink alcohol to excess, fight or quarrel?

Did I physically injure or kill anyone?

Have I had or advised anyone to have an abortion?

Did I participate in or approve of the grave evil known as "mercy killing" or euthanasia?

Did I attempt suicide?

Did I willfully entertain impure thoughts and desires?

Did I dress immodestly?

Did I use impure or suggestive words?

Did I tell impure stories or listen to them?

Did I deliberately look at impure television, Internet, plays, pictures or movies?

Did I deliberately read impure material?

Did I perform impure acts by myself (masturbation) or with another (adultery, fornication or sodomy)?

Did I marry or advise another to marry outside of the Church?

Did I abuse my marriage rights?

Was I unfaithful to my marriage vows?

Have I kept company with someone else's spouse?

Did I practice artificial birth control or was I or my spouse permanently sterilized (tubal ligation or vasectomy)?

Did I steal, cheat, help or encourage others to steal or keep stolen goods?

Have I made restitution for stolen goods?

Did I fulfill my contracts, give or accept bribes, pay my bills, rashly gamble or speculate or deprive my family of the necessities of life?

Did I tell lies? Deliberately in order to deceive or injure others?

Did I commit perjury?

Did I vote in accordance with a properly informed conscience, in a way consistent with the teachings of the Church, in regard to the sanctity of human life and human life issues?

Was I uncharitable in word or deed?

Did I gossip or reveal the faults and sins of others?

Did I fail to keep secrets that I should have kept?

Did I eat meat on the Fridays during Lent or on Ash Wednesday?

Did I fast as required on Ash Wednesday and Good Friday?

Did I fail to receive Holy Communion during the Easter Season?

Did I fail to confess my sins at least once a year?

Did I go to Holy Communion in the state of mortal sin?

Did I go to Holy Communion without fasting for one hour or more from food and drink (water and medicine are permitted)?

Did I make a bad Confession?

Did I deliberately not tell all the sins I committed during one of my Confessions?

Did I fail to contribute to the support of the Church?

How to go to Confession

1. The priest will greet you.

2. The penitent says: "Forgive me, Father, for I have sinned." You then say how long it has been since your last Confession.

3. The penitent tells the priest his sins and answers any questions.

4. The priest will give you some advice and will assign you a penance.

5. The penitent will next pray the Act of Contrition (see prayer below).

6. The priest then gives the penitent absolution.

7. The priest will then say: "Give thanks to the Lord, for He is good."

8. The penitent responds: "His mercy endures for ever." The priest will then dismiss you.

Act of Contrition

O my God, I am heartily sorry for having offended thee. And I detest all my sins because of thy just punishment, but most of all because they offend thee my God, who are all good and deserving of all my love. I firmly resolve, with the help of thy grace, to sin no more and to avoid the near occasion of sin. — Amen!

Prayer After Confession

Almighty and Merciful God, Whose mercy is boundless and everlasting and of Whose goodness the riches are infinite, I thank You because You have so graciously pardoned all my sins and restored Your Heavenly favor. I am awed by Your divine compassion and the incomprehensible love of Your Son, which has led Him to institute so gentle and powerful a remedy for sins. In union with all the gratitude that has ever ascended to You from truly penitent hearts, I proclaim Your merciful praises on behalf of all in Heaven, on Earth and in purgatory, for ever and ever. —Amen.

[Taken from http://www.newmanconnection.com/ccwatershed/Examination.pdf]

Section 2

The Prayer of Daniel 6:11

"Even after Daniel heard that this law had been signed, he continued his custom of going home to kneel in prayer and give thanks to his God in the upper chamber, three times a day, with the windows open toward Jerusalem."

—Daniel 6:11

3-Second Daily Prayers

Monday: *(World Peace)* Dear Jesus, Prince of Peace, bring peace to persons, families and nations everywhere — Amen.

Tuesday: *(The Homeless)* Dear Jesus, you were born homeless. Have pity on all without shelter or warmth today — Amen.

Wednesday: *(The Physically & Emotionally ill)* Dear Jesus, heal all the sick who are now suffering in body, mind or spirit — Amen.

Thursday: *(Abused Children)* Dear Jesus, comfort your little ones, who are abused in mind, body or spirit, please heal them — Amen.

Friday: *(The Chemically Addicted)* Dear Jesus, by your thirst on the cross normalize and regulate all the disordered appetites of your children and bring them to a life of sobriety — Amen.

Saturday: *(Vocations)* Dear Jesus, Lord of the harvest, send many holy and consecrated laborers into your vineyard — Amen.

Sunday: *(Spiritual Growth)* Oh Holy Spirit, Sanctifier of souls, grace our souls with the holiness of God — Amen.

Morning Daily Prayers

"Every morning we arise afresh in Christ our light. Ancient Christian writers warn against 'morning demons': yesterdays worries and grievances returning to poison the new day."[24]

"We should begin each day with prayers that consecrate our thoughts, our actions, and our very souls to the Lordship and Kingship of Jesus Christ through the intercession of our Queen Mother. This sets the tempo for the rest of the day…"

—Jesse Romero

Morning Offering

O Jesus, Through the Immaculate Heart of Mary, I offer you my prayers, works, joys and sufferings of this day in union with the Holy Sacrifice of the Mass throughout the world. I offer them for the intentions of your most Sacred Heart, the salvation of souls, reparation for sin, the reunion of all Christians. I offer them for the intentions of our bishops and all the apostles of prayer, and in particular for those recommended by our Holy Father this month. — Amen.

Dedication To Jesus

Take Lord and receive all my liberty, my memory, my understanding and my entire will, all that I have and possess. You have given all to me. To you O Lord I return it. All is yours, dispose of it according to your Holy will. Give me your love and your grace, for this is sufficient for me. — Amen.

Spiritual Communion With Jesus

My Jesus, I believe that thou are present in the Most Blessed Sacrament. I love Thee above all things, and I desire to possess Thee within my soul. Since I unable now to receive you sacramentally, come at least spiritually into my heart. I embrace Thee as being already there and I unite myself wholly and entirely to thee. — Amen.

Consecration to our Blessed Mother

My Queen! My Mother! I give myself entirely to you, and to show my devotion to you, I consecrate to you this day, my eyes, my ears, my mouth, my heart, my whole being without reserve. Wherefore, most loving Mother, as I am your own, keep me, defend me, as your property and possession. — Amen.

Our Father

Our Father, who art in Heaven, hallowed be Thy name; Thy Kingdom come, Thy will be done on Earth as it is in Heaven. Give us this day our daily bread; and forgive us our trespasses as we forgive those who trespass against us; and lead us not into temptation, but deliver us from evil. — Amen.

Hail Mary

Hail Mary, Full of Grace, The Lord is with thee. Blessed art thou among women, and blessed is the fruit of thy womb, Jesus. Holy Mary, Mother of God, pray for us sinners now, and at the hour of our death. — Amen.

(3 times for her intercessory protection against the devil, the world, the flesh and for an increase of faith, hope and love).

Anima Cristi

Soul of Christ, sanctify me. Body of Christ, save me. Blood of Christ, inebriate me. Water from the side of Christ, wash me. Passion of Christ, strengthen me. Oh Good Jesus, hear me. Within your wounds, hide me. Separated from you let me never be, from the evil one, protect me. At the hour of my death, call me. And close to you keep me, that with your saints and angels I may praise you forever and ever. — Amen.

Fatima Prayer

My God, I believe I adore I trust and I love you. I beg pardon for all those who do not believe do not adore, do not trust and do not love you. Oh Most Holy Trinity — Father, Son and Holy Spirit — I adore you profoundly. I offer you the most precious Body, Blood, Soul and Divinity of our Lord Jesus Christ, present in all the tabernacles of the world, in reparation for the outrages, sacrileges and indifferences by which He is offended. By the infinite merits of the Most Sacred Heart of Jesus and the Immaculate Heart of Mary, I beg of thee the conversion of poor sinners. — Amen.

Miraculous Medal Prayer

O Mary conceived without sin, pray for us who have recourse to thee.

Memorare

Remember, O most gracious Virgin Mary, that never was it known that anyone who fled to thy protection, implored thy help, or sought thy intercession was left unaided. Inspired by this confidence, I fly unto thee, O Virgin of virgins, my Mother; to thee do I come; before thee I stand, sinful and sorrowful. O Mother of the Word Incarnate, despise not my petitions, but in thy mercy hear us and answer us. — Amen.

St. Michael Prayer

St. Michael the Archangel defend us in battle. Be our protection against the wickedness and snares of the devil. May God rebuke him we humbly pray and do thou, O Prince of the heavenly host, by the power of God, cast into Hell Satan and all the evil spirits who prowl about the world seeking the ruin of souls. — Amen.

Guardian Angel Prayer

Angel of God, my guardian dear, to whom the love of God commits me here, be ever this day be at my side, to light, to guard, to rule and to guide. — Amen.

Prayer to the Holy Spirit

O Holy Spirit, beloved of my soul, I adore you. Enlighten me, guide me, strengthen me, console me. Tell me what I should do, give me Your orders. I promise to submit myself to all that You desire of me and to accept all that You permit to happen to me. Let me only know your will. — Amen.

Glory Be

Glory be to the Father, and to the Son and to the Holy Spirit, as it was in the beginning, is now, and ever shall be, world without end. — Amen.

(3 times in praise of the Holy Trinity).

Closing Prayer

Praise you Lord Jesus Christ – Now and forever.

Jesus, Mary, and Joseph – we love you save souls.

Jesus live in our hearts – forever.

Jesus – I trust in you.

We cover ourselves with the precious blood of Jesus and put on the full armor of God in the name of the Father, and of the Son and of the Holy Spirit — Amen.

Mid-Day Prayers

"When we pause our lives to pray in the middle of the day, we place Jesus at the center of our life and Our Lord knows we are serious about our faith."

—Jesse Romero

The Angelus (12 noon)

The Angel of the Lord declared unto Mary:
R: And she conceived by the Holy Spirit. Hail Mary, full of grace….

Behold the handmaid of the Lord:
R: Be it done unto me according to Thy word. Hail Mary, full of grace…

And the Word was made Flesh:
R: And dwelt among us. Hail Mary, full of grace…

Pray for us, O Holy Mother of God:
R: That we may be made worthy of the promises of Christ.

Let us pray: Pour forth, we beseech Thee, O Lord, Thy grace into our hearts; that we, to whom the incarnation of Christ, Thy Son, was made known to us by the message of an angel, may by His Passion and Cross be brought to the glory of His Resurrection, through the same Christ Our Lord — Amen.

Divine Mercy Chaplet

(3pm — Jesus says this is the hour of mercy — he died for our sins at this hour).

You expired, Jesus, but the source of life opened up for souls, and the ocean of mercy opened up for the world. O fount of life, unfathomable Divine Mercy, envelop the whole world and empty yourself out upon us.

O Blood and water which gushed forth from the heart of Jesus as a fountain of mercy for us, I trust in You! *(3 times).*

1 Our Father

1 Hail Mary

The Apostles' Creed

On the Our Father Beads say the following:

Eternal Father, I offer You the Body and Blood, Soul and Divinity of Your dearly beloved Son, Our Lord Jesus Christ, in atonement for our sins and for those of the whole world.

On the 10 Hail Mary Beads say the following:

For the sake of His sorrowful Passion, have mercy on us and on the whole world.

(Repeat step 2 and 3 for all five decades).

Conclude with:

Holy God, Holy Mighty One, Holy Immortal One, have mercy on us and on the whole world *(3 times).*

Eternal God, in whom mercy is endless and the treasury of compassion inexhaustible, look kindly upon us and increase Your mercy in us, that in difficult moments we might not despair nor come despondent, but with great confidence submit ourselves to Your holy will, which is Love and Mercy itself.

Jesus, I trust in you *(3 times)*

Make the sign of the Cross (and pray)

In the name of the Father and of the Son and of the Holy Spirit — Amen.

Evening & Night Prayers

"...Evening prayers should be said after a reflection of the day (known as an examination of conscience). The leader of the household should encourage all those present to pause and give thanks to the Lord for another day of life. At this time, the needs of the family should be brought to the foot of the cross..."

—Jesse Romero

"Nightfall can be the moment at which all the evils of the day, real and imagined, crowd around and beset us, as the storm beset the disciples on the sea. All we need to do is call upon Christ our light, and he will come and say to us: 'Do not be Afraid.'"[25]

Lovely Lady Dressed in Blue

Lovely Lady dressed in blue, teach me how to pray, God was just your little boy, tell me what to say. Did you lift him up high gently on your knee? Did you sing to him the way mother does to me? Did you hold his hand at night? Did you ever try telling him stories of the world? Oh! And did he cry? Do you really think he cares if I tell him things, little things that happen? And do the angel's wings make a noise? And can he hear me if I speak low? Does he understand me now? Tell me, for you know. Lovely Lady dressed in blue, teach me how to pray, God was just your little boy and you know the way — Amen.

Next, (take a minute of silence) examine your conscience, then say an:

Act of Contrition

O my God, I am heartily sorry for having offended thee. And I detest all my sins because of thy just punishment, but most of all because they offend thee my God, who are all good and deserving of all my love. I firmly resolve, with the help of thy grace, to sin no more and to avoid the near occasion of sin. — Amen!

Night Prayer #1

Now I lay me down to sleep, I pray the Lord my soul to keep. If I should die before I wake, I pray the Lord my soul to take — Amen.

Night Prayer #2

Protect us Lord as we stay awake, and watch over us as we sleep. That awake we may keep watch with Christ, and asleep we may rest in His peace — Amen.

Night Prayer #3

Visit Oh Lord this habitation and drive far from it all snares of the enemy; Let thy holy angels dwell therein, and may thy blessing be upon us through Christ our Lord — Amen.

St. Michael Prayer

St. Michael the Archangel defend us in battle. Be our protection against the wickedness and snares of the devil. May God rebuke him we humbly pray and do thou, O Prince of the heavenly host, by the power of God, cast into Hell Satan and all the evil spirits who prowl about the world seeking the ruin of souls — Amen.

Guardian Angel Prayer

Angel of God, my guardian dear, to whom the love of God commits me here, be ever this NIGHT at my side to light, to guard, to rule and to guide — Amen.

Anima Christi

Soul of Christ, sanctify me. Body of Christ, save me. Blood of Christ, inebriate me. Water from the side of Christ, wash me. Passion of Christ, strengthen me. Oh Good Jesus, hear me. Within your wounds, hide me. Separated from you let me never be, from the evil one, protect me. At the hour of my death, call me. And close to you bid me, that with your saints and angels I may praise you forever and ever — Amen.

"Into Your Hands Lord, I commit my spirit."

—Psalm 31: 5

I Consecrate My House

Most Blessed Virgin, whose Heart is Sorrowful and Immaculate, we recognize Thee as the Lady and Queen of this house.

Have the kindness to preserve it from any evil; from fire, water, thunder, storms, earthquakes, from robbers, wicked people, from revolutions, war, raids, from persecution and taxes, from any other evil known by Thee.

Bless, protect, defend and preserve as Thy personal property, those who live and will live here. Keep them from adversity and misfortune, but above all, preserve them from offending God. Let not a single mortal sin be ever committed in this house. And may all those who enter it work for the Glory of God, for the Reign of Jesus and Mary.

Let this house be forever consecrated to You, O Jesus and Mary. Let it be blessed with all those who inhabit it — Amen.

[During the 1st World War, in France, some of the faithful Catholics were known to have this prayer tacked on their front door. These homes and residents were not harmed or invaded during the time of war].

Closing Prayers

Praise you Lord Jesus Christ – Now and forever.

Jesus, Mary, and Joseph – we love you save souls.

Jesus live in our hearts – forever.

Jesus – I trust in you.

We cover ourselves with the precious blood of Jesus and cover ourselves with the full armor of God in the name of the Father, and of the Son and of the Holy Spirit — Amen.

The Most Holy Rosary

The Holy Rosary is like a spiritual 50 caliber machine gun in your hands. The beads are like silver bullets for the spiritual battle. The rosary in your hands is like a slingshot in Davids hands (cf.1 Samuel 17). Read how that turned out for Goliath.

In the name of The Father, and of the Son and of the Holy Spirit — Amen.

The Apostles Creed

I believe in God, the Father almighty, Creator of Heaven and Earth, and in Jesus Christ, His only Son, our Lord. He was conceived by the Holy Spirit, born of the Virgin Mary, suffered under Pontius Pilate, was crucified, died and was buried. He descended into Hell. On the third day He rose again from the dead; he ascended into Heaven, and is seated at the right hand of God the Father Almighty; from there he will come again to judge the living and the dead. I believe in the Holy Spirit, the holy Catholic Church, the communion of saints, the forgiveness of sins, the resurrection of the body, and life everlasting — Amen.

Say: 1 "Our Father", 3 "Hail Mary's" (Faith, Hope and Charity), 1 "Glory Be."

After each decade of the Holy Rosary, the "Fatima Prayer" is said: O my Jesus, forgive us our sins, save us from the fires of Hell, lead all souls to Heaven, especially those who are in most need of thy mercy.

The Joyful Mysteries

(Mondays and Saturdays, may be said on Sundays during Advent and Christmas)

1. **The Annunciation** – Luke 1:26-28; *pray for the love of humility*

2. **The Visitation** – Luke 1:39-41; *pray for charity towards my neighbor*

3. **The Nativity** – Luke 2:7; *pray for the spirit of poverty*

4. **The Presentation** – Luke 2:27-30; *pray for virtue of obedience*

5. **The Finding of Jesus in the Temple** – Luke 2:46-47; *pray for virtue of piety*

The Sorrowful Mysteries

(Tuesdays and Fridays, Sundays during Lent)

1. **The Agony in the Garden** – Matthew 26:36-44; *pray for true contrition for your sins*

2. **The Scourging at the Pillar** – Mark 15:15; *pray for the virtue of purity*

3. **The Crowning with Thorns** – John 19:2-3; *pray for moral courage*

4. **The Carrying of the Cross** – John 19:17; *pray for the virtue of patience*

5. **The Crucifixion** – Luke 23:33-34; *pray for final perseverance*

The Glorious Mysteries

(Wednesdays and Sundays)

1. **The Resurrection** – John 20:8-9; *pray for the virtue of faith*

2. **The Ascension** – Luke 24:50-51; *pray for the virtue of hope*

3. **The Descent of the Holy Spirit** – Acts 2:3-4; *pray for the virtue of love*

4. **The Assumption of the Blessed Virgin Mary** – Judith 13:18; Psalm 132:8, Revelation 11:19; *pray for a happy death*

5. **The Coronation of the Blessed Virgin Mary** – Revelation 12:1; *pray for eternal salvation*

The Luminous Mysteries

(Thursdays)

1. **The Baptism in the Jordan** – Matthew 3:16; *pray for submission to God' will*

2. **The Wedding at Cana** – John 2:1-11; *pray for devotion to Mary*

3. **Proclamation of the Kingdom** – Mark 1:14-15 *pray for the grace of conversion*

4. **The Transfiguration** – Matthew 17:1-2; *pray for fear of God*

5. **Institution of the Eucharist** – Matthew 26:26; *praise and give thanks to God*

Hail Holy Queen

After completion of the Rosary, the "Hail Holy Queen" is said:

Hail, holy Queen, mother of mercy, our life, our sweetness, and our hope. To thee do we cry, poor banished children of Eve. To thee do we send up our sighs mourning and weeping in this valley of tears. Turn then, most gracious advocate, thine eyes of mercy toward us, and after this our exile show unto us the blessed fruit of thy womb, Jesus. O clement, O loving, O sweet Virgin Mary, Pray for us, O Holy Mother of God; that we may be made worthy of the promises of Christ.

Let us pray, O God, whose only begotten Son, by His life, death, and resurrection, has purchased the rewards of eternal salvation. Grant we beseech thee, that while meditating on these mysteries of the most holy Rosary of the Blessed Virgin Mary, that we may both imitate what they contain and obtain what they promise, through Christ our Lord — Amen.

Most Sacred Heart of Jesus, have mercy on us.

Immaculate Heart of Mary, pray for us.

Litanies To Our Lady of Loreto

Our Lady is a 12-star General, she has big combat boots, she has been given power and authority by God to crush the head of Satan the serpent (cf. Genesis 3:15).

Litany of Loreto

V. Lord, have mercy.
R. Christ have mercy.
V. Lord have mercy. Christ hear us.
R. Christ graciously hear us.
God the Father of Heaven, *have mercy on us.*
God the Son, Redeemer of the world, *have mercy on us.*
God the Holy Spirit, *have mercy on us.*
Holy Trinity, one God, *have mercy on us.*

Holy Mary, *pray for us.*
Holy Mother of God, *pray for us.*
Holy Virgin of Virgins, [*etc.*]
Mother of Christ,
Mother of divine grace,
Mother most pure,
Mother most chaste,
Mother inviolate,
Mother undefiled,
Mother most amiable,
Mother most admirable,
Mother of good Counsel,
Mother of our Creator,
Mother of our Savior,
Virgin most prudent,
Virgin most venerable,
Virgin most renowned,
Virgin most powerful,

Virgin most merciful,
Virgin most faithful,
Mirror of justice,
Seat of wisdom,
Cause of our joy,
Spiritual vessel,
Vessel of honor,
Singular vessel of devotion,
Mystical rose,
Tower of David,
Tower of ivory,
House of gold,
Ark of the covenant,
Gate of Heaven,
Morning star,
Health of the sick,
Refuge of sinners,
Comforter of the afflicted,
Help of Christians,
Queen of Angels,
Queen of Patriarchs,
Queen of Prophets,
Queen of Apostles,
Queen of Martyrs,
Queen of Confessors,
Queen of Virgins,
Queen of all Saints,
Queen conceived without original sin,
Queen assumed into Heaven,
Queen of the most holy Rosary,
Queen of families,
Queen of peace,

V. Lamb of God, Who takest away the sins of the world,
R. Spare us, O Lord.
V. Lamb of God, Who takest away the sins of the world,
R. Graciously hear us, O Lord.

V. Lamb of God, Who takest away the sins of the world,
Have mercy on us.

V. Pray for us, O holy Mother of God.
R. That we may be made worthy of the promises of Christ.

Let us pray. Grant, we beseech Thee, O Lord God, that we thy servants may enjoy perpetual health of mind and body, and by the glorious intercession of blessed Mary, ever Virgin, may we be freed from present sorrow, and rejoice in eternal happiness. Through Christ our Lord —Amen.

How to Read the Bible *(Lectio Divina)*

"If modern Catholics want to develop a fruitful prayer life, they need to go 'old school' with their approach. Prayer is not an activity that comes about easily. It is essentially a conversation with God, but our speaking to God is only half the conversation. The other half must come as God speaks to us. The problem is that many do not know how to hear God when He is speaking. Through the ancient practice of Lectio Divina *we learn how Scripture opens up to us this other half of the dialogue of prayer."*

— Dr. Tim Gray
Author of *Praying Scripture for a Change: An Introduction of Lectio Divina*

"I would like in particular to recall and recommend the ancient tradition of Lectio Divina, *if it is effectively promoted, this practice will bring to the Church, I am convinced, a new spiritual springtime."*

— Pope Benedict XVI
Universal Synod, Rome, Oct. 2008

"Once Christians learn to practice Lectio Divina *their eyes will be opened to an amazing reality, God is speaking directly to them through the Holy Scriptures."*

—Dr. Tim Gray

"When we pray, we speak to God; when we read Scripture, God speaks to us." The key to enriching our prayer is learning the language of Christianity, and the most effective way to learn the language of Christianity is an ancient technique known as Lectio Divina *(divine reading.)*

—St. Augustine

Lets explore the 4 rungs that make up *Lectio Divina,* steps that will help ordinary laymen to become extraordinary saints by learning this ancient, yet amazingly simple method of prayer.

But first let's look at—THE PRAYER EXPERIENCE — that I will walk you through has 3 distinct parts, they are:

- Quiet & Focused Prayer
- *Lectio Divina*
- Mental Prayer

Quiet & Focusing Prayer

This is simply asking the Lord to take away distractions. Allowing the Holy Spirit to quiet the mind and drive away anything that would keep you from giving God your full attention – things such as fear, anxiety, doubt, stress, and temptations. You willfully give yourself completely to God and ask Him to take these things. Then you say nothing. If anything comes to your mind or heart, turn it over to God. Say, "Lord I give you this thought, this pain, this struggle, this emotion that just came to my mind and heart. A good prayer to say during this time would be:

St. Ignatius Consecration

Take Lord and receive all my liberty, my memory my

understanding and my entire will. All that I have and possess you have given all to me. To you Oh Lord I return it. All is yours, dispose of it according to your holy will. Give me your love and your grace for this is sufficient for me.

Lectio Divina

Because prayer is conversation, we let God speak first through *Lectio Divina. Lectio divina* is a very ancient art, practiced by all Christians. It is a slow, contemplative praying of the Scriptures which enables the Bible, the Word of God, to become a means of union with God. It infuses the Word of God into our daily life. Here is an example of *Lectio Divina*: Psalm 1:1-2 "Blessed is the man who walks not in the counsel of the wicked, nor stands in the way of sinners, nor sits in the seat of scoffers; but his delight is in the law of the Lord, and on his law he meditates day and night."

There are 4 steps to the *Lectio Divina* exercise (Read, Reflect, Respond, & Rest).

1. **Lectio (Read):** The reading of and listening to Scripture. It is a slow, repetitive and deliberate. It involves all the senses and times of silence in between the readings. As you read you ask: "What does the text say?"

2. **Mediation or Meditation (Reflect):** We let the Holy Spirit guide us to a particular word or idea in the scripture reading and we spend time chewing on it. We ponder it. We stay focused on it and let the Spirit open it up for us. We ask, "What do I think?"

3. **Oratio or Prayer (Respond)**: In the next step, you take the Scripture and use it in a loving conversation with God. You take the word you have meditated on and let it touch and consecrate a part of your heart to

God. Leave your thinking aside and listen with your heart to what God is saying to you.

4. ***Contemplatio* or Contemplation (Rest):** Finally, you simply rest in the presence of God, who has used His word as a means of inviting us to accept His transforming embrace. We practice silence, letting go of our words; this time simply enjoying the experience of being in the presence of God and silently resting with the Word of God.

Mental Prayer

Finally, after being in union with God we respond as the Holy Spirit leads us. This is our mental prayer because it is our minds that lead our hearts and wills to deeper devotion to Christ and conformity to His will. Mental prayer could be repentance, praise, petitions, or even prayers of commitment. Or if the Spirit is moving, elements of all those things. You can use formal prayers and spontaneous prayer. During this time it is important to raise our hearts and minds to God and bend our wills toward the direction the Holy Spirit prompts us. Here is an appropriate prayer for this exercise:

Come Holy Spirit, fill the hearts of your faithful and kindle in them the fire of your love.

V. Send forth your Spirit, and they shall be created.
R. And You shall renew the face of the Earth.

Let us pray. O, God, who by the light of the Holy Spirit, did instruct the hearts of the faithful, grant that by the same Holy Spirit we may be truly wise and ever enjoy His consolations, through Christ Our Lord — Amen.

If *Lectio Divina* is done with a group here is the way it should be done. The overall flow of the prayer experience will be:

1. Lead them to silence by inviting the Holy Spirit to come and take distractions away (1-2 minutes).

2. Lead them through the *Lectio Divina* exercise (10 min).

3. Have them finish with 2-3 minutes of silent mental prayer.

4. Give them 15 minutes to discuss the experience with one another.

For the purpose of the Sunday morning Gospel reading the *Lectio Divina* exercise should flow like this:

1. Sunday's Gospel should be read out loud 3 times with a minute of silence in between each time its read. Each time it is read slowly and deliberately.

2. Ask the participants to meditate upon the words and have them pick out the word or phrase that most touches their heart and take that to prayer. This prayer should last 2-3 minutes.

3. After the prayer, have them circle with others around them and briefly share what it was God said to their heart.

4. After a couple of minutes of sharing, refocus the group by proclaiming the Gospel again and have them sit for 3-5 minutes of silence with the Word of God.

Lectio Divina is not a Bible Study course, this ancient practice is not meant to make you a Bible scholar, it will make you become a Bible lover. *Lectio Divina* should be practiced by new Catholics, lifelong Catholics, Non-Catholics, Revert Catholics and all Catholic Christians.

Section 3

Engaged in the Battle

"Demons are primary evil, humans are secondary evil. Demons use humans as their useful idiots, they prey upon our fallen nature."

—Jesse Romero

"When I am asked how many demons there are, I answer with the words that the demon himself spoke through a demoniac: 'We are so many that, if we were visible, we would darken the sun.'"

—Fr Gabriel Amorth, Chief Exorcist of the Vatican

Know the Enemy

There is one verse in the Holy Bible which describes the Devil's strategy on how he tries to turn us into Secular Humanist, Moral-Relativist, Hedonist, Carnalist, Narcissist, Liberal Progressive, Idolaters.

"Do not love the world or the things in the world. If anyone loves the world, love for the Father is not in him. For all that is in the world, the lust of the flesh (pleasures – lust) and the lust of the eyes (possessions – greed) and the pride of life (pride – arrogance, hubris), is not of the Father but is of the world. And the world passes away, and the lust of it; but he who does the will of God abides forever."

—1 John 2:15-17

We must evaluate what life throws are way and say "Yes" to things that have eternal value and say "No" to those which have only temporal value and merely carnal pleasure. Risking eternal treasure (Heaven) for temporary trash is a bad trade off.

Three Front Warfare: The Devil, the World & the Flesh

> *"Men, we must never believe that holiness and courage are things of the past! You and I are called to a holiness that shows Christ to the world as our forefathers have done countless times throughout history, following the inspiration of the Holy Spirit. Indeed, in this time of evil's growing boldness, each man must prepare himself for nothing less than martyrdom, whatever form this may take, and to instill in his children and grandchildren the willingness to do the same."*[26]
>
> —Bishop Thomas Olmsted

The Devil (*Pride*)**:** Preternatural attacks from the devil or his demons are usually directed to our mind (cf. Acts 5:3; 2 Corinthians 11:3). This is known as "demonic thought tampering."[27] Although demonic attacks can be physical (cf. Luke 13:10-11), demonic attacks are described in Sacred Scripture as being shot with "flaming arrows" (Ephesians 6:16). These attacks can be in the form of annoying accusations to make the victim weak and fearful (Revelation 12:10-11). Demonic attacks can also be internal (obsession) or external (oppression) or even the invasion of a house or location by demons (infestation). "Pride" is the most dangerous of the 7 Deadly Sins because it blinds one's understanding and makes one boastful and self-centered. St. Thomas Aquinas says Satan's original sin was "pride".[28] The devil is named our arch enemy (cf. John 8:44; 1 Peter 5:8; 2 Corinthians 4:4; Matthew 4:1; Revelation 12:10).

The World (*Greed*)**:** The World (of unbelievers is controlled by the devil). In this context, 'world' refers to nations in rebellion against God by unbelievers who are in power and have set up "social structures of sin."[29] The attacks are external in nature. In 1 John 2:15-17, scripture indicates that temptations from the world attack us through the lust of the flesh which is designed to trigger our disordered passions. This causes us to have insatiable disordered appetites for "more – more." This is known as the sin of "avarice" (CCC #1866) or the sin of "coveting" (Exodus 20:17). "Do not store up for yourselves treasures on Earth, where moths and vermin destroy, and where thieves break in and steal. But store up for yourselves treasures in Heaven, where moths and vermin do not destroy, and where thieves do not break in and steal. For where your treasure is, there your heart will be also" (Matthew 6:19-21). "Greed" is a disordered passion wherein we seek and worship the temporal and transitory, and neglect the eternal. Unbelievers are not our enemies, the "world" of unbelievers is our enemy. And I repeat, the world is controlled by Satan himself (cf. Ephesians 2:2; John 12:31; 1 John 5:19).

The Flesh (*Lust*)**:** Spiritual Warfare against the flesh can also trigger physiological responses within our mind and body thereby triggering our appetites to be disordered. The "lust of the eyes" is designed to manipulate, pervert and reduce our love of true beauty, to the point of idolatry. This type of demonic attack is internal. Our concupiscence, i.e. our inclination to evil as a result of our wounded nature, and our sense appetites (our lower faculties), wars against our intellect and will which are the higher faculties (cf. Romans 7:15-25; Galatians 5:17). The biblical response to attacks of the flesh, is to flee from the temptation (cf. 2 Timothy 2:22). In other words, take custody of your senses and avoid the "near occasion" of sin. This admonition is written in the "act of contrition" prayer. Fr Gabriel Amorth (Vatican Exorcist) says that "Satan uses the idolatry of sex, which reduces the human body to an instrument of sin."[30] This attack on our flesh is confirmed by Sacred Scripture (cf. 1 Thessalonians

3:5; 1 Timothy 5:15; Romans 7:18-19; 1 Corinthians 2:14-15 [unspiritual men]; 1 Corinthians 3:1-3 [Men of the Flesh]).

> *"We must watch over our mind, our hearts, and our senses, for these are the gates by which the devil enters in."*[31]
>
> —St. John Vianney

There are two things we, as Christians, will have to fight until the Lord calls us home; one is Satan and the other is our "*fomes peccati*" (tinder to sin) or "concupiscence." This is described clearly in Romans 7:14-24.

> *"For all sin at its roots is an abandonment of our heavenly Father for the pursuit of freedom and pleasure."*
>
> —CCC #397

> *"Mortal sin...results in the loss...of sanctifying grace. If it is not redeemed by repentance and God's forgiveness, it causes exclusion from Christ's kingdom and the eternal death of Hell…"*
>
> —CCC #1861

If we die in unrepentant mortal sin our soul will go to Hell upon death! The Holy Eucharist is the medicine of immortality and the antidote against sin. Perfect contrition would compel us to go to Holy Mass out of love for God, imperfect contrition would compel us to go to Holy Mass out of fear of Hell.

> *"Therefore Lord we pray: graciously accept this oblation of our service, that of your whole family; order our days in your peace, and command that we be delivered from eternal damnation and counted among the flock of those you have chosen…"*
>
> —Eucharist Prayer 1

"…and lead us not into temptation but deliver us from evil" (most manuscripts say, "evil one", this is a direct reference to the devil).

—Lords Prayer

"Deliver Lord, we pray, from every evil graciously grant peace in our days…"

—Priestly Prayer

"O my Jesus, forgive us our sins, save us from the fires of Hell, lead all souls to Heaven especially those in most need of thy mercy."

—Fatima Prayer

O MY GOD, I am heartily sorry for having offended Thee, and I detest all my sins because I dread the loss of Heaven and the pains of Hell; but most of all because they offend Thee, my God, Who art all-good and deserving of all my love. I firmly resolve, with the help of Thy grace, to confess my sins, to do penance, and to amend my life —Amen."

—Traditional Act of Contrition

Repent, Renounce, Resist, & Renew
4 R's To Overcome the Devil

CS. Lewis (*Screwtape Letters*) in Letter VII, Screwtape a senior demon tells his young protégé (a junior demon) that the most effective thing he can do to bring souls to Hell is to convince people that Satan does not even exist.

If Satan's stronghold (cf. 2 Corinthians 10:4) is to be broken, 4 steps need to be taken in order to get him out: REPENT, RENOUNCE, RESIST, and RENEW your mind.

1. Repentance

> *"Repent and believe in the Gospel…"*
>
> —Mark 1:15

> *"…Repent, and be baptized every one of you in the name of Jesus Christ for the forgiveness of your sins…"*
>
> —Acts 2: 38

Here are 5 examples of how to do this. These prayers must be said with a contrite[32] heart:

i. **Penitential Rite** (Mass): I confess to almighty God and to you, my brothers and sisters, that I have sinned through my own fault (we strike our breast; cf. Luke 18:13) in my thoughts and in my words, in what I have done, and in what I have failed to do; and I ask blessed Mary, ever virgin, all the angels and saints, and you, my brothers and sisters, to pray for me to the Lord our God.

Priest: May almighty God have mercy on us, forgive us our sins, and bring us to everlasting life — Amen.

ii. **The Kyrie** (Holy Mass): Lord, have mercy; Lord, have mercy. Christ, have mercy: Christ, have mercy. Lord, have mercy; Lord, have mercy. May almighty God have mercy on us, forgive us our sins, and bring us to everlasting life — Amen.

iii. **Fatima Prayer:** O My Jesus, forgive us our sins, save us from the fires of Hell, lead all souls to Heaven, especially those who are in most need of Thy mercy.

iv. **Act of Contrition:** O my God, I am heartily sorry for having offended Thee, and I detest all my sins because of Thy just punishments, but most of all because they offend Thee my God, Who art all-good and deserving of all my love. I firmly resolve, with the help of Thy grace, to sin no more and to avoid the near occasions of sin.

v. **Jesus Prayer** (CCC #435): Lord Jesus Christ, Son of God, have mercy on me, a sinner.[33]

We have the power to destroy demonic/sinful strongholds (cf. 2 Corinthians 10:4) by going often to the sacrament of confession, turning away from our sins, receiving the Holy Eucharist every Sunday and praying everyday.

2. Renounce

"When the Church asks publicly and authoritatively in the name of Jesus Christ that a person or object be protected against the power of the 'Evil One' and withdrawn from his dominion, it is called exorcism. Jesus performed exorcisms and from him the Church has received the power and office of exorcizing. In a simple form, exorcism is performed at the celebration of Baptism."(CCC #1673) A Catholic Priest or Deacon performs a simple Exorcism over us during our own Baptism. Here is what was prayed over us:

> *"Almighty and ever-living God, you sent your only Son into the world to cast out the power of Satan, spirit of evil, to rescue man from the kingdom of darkness, and bring him into the splendor of your kingdom of light. We pray for this child, set him (her) free from original sin, make him (her) a temple of your glory, and send your Holy Spirit to dwell with him (her). We ask this through Christ our Lord."*

Baptism is the 1st line of defense against the demonic (cf. CCC #1673). Fr Ripperger F.S.S.P. (Exorcist) said that when baptisms and Church weddings decrease in society – demonic activity increases, the decline in morality of a society accompanies an increase in demonic activity.[34]

Infant baptism has dropped by 28%, adult baptism has dropped by 31%, and sacramental marriages have dropped by 41%. This is a serious breach, a gaping hole in Christ's battle lines.[35]

Pope Francis said in his first homily as Pope (in the Sistine Chapel on March 14, 2013) when he said Mass for the College of Cardinals. He warned these princes of the church against professing what he called "the worldliness of the devil, a demonic worldliness."

On Feb 23, 2015 Cardinal Francis Xavier Kriengsak Kovithavanij of Bangkok, Thailand boldly said that all the world is facing the challenge of secularism, he called *secularism the devil's face in the modern world. Secularism is the new way the devil presents himself in the modern world, he added that the devilish force takes an attractive appearance, rather than a grotesque one.*

Fr. Vince Lampert, also an exorcist, said: "...the increase in demonic activity is not merely because the devil has 'upped his game,' but also because more people are willing to play his game today, through activities that are opening up doorways to evil in their lives."[36]

Also, at least once a year, Catholic Christians reaffirm our baptismal promises during Holy Mass at Easter. We stand and the Priest asks us:

> Priest: Do you reject Satan and all his works?
> *Response: I do.*
>
> Priest: Do you reject sin, so as to live in the freedom of God's children?
> *Response: I do.*
>
> Priest: Do you reject the glamor of evil, and refuse to be mastered by sin?
> *Response: I do.*
>
> Priest: Do you reject Satan, father of sin and prince of darkness?
> *Response: I do.*

Example of Renunciation Prayer

In the powerful Name of Jesus, I renounce any occult spirits picked up through occult practices that continue to harm and control me; I refuse to live under their power any longer. Come Most Sovereign Mistress of the Holy Angels and Mistress of the Most Holy Rosary, thou who from the very beginning hast received from God the power and the mission to crush the head of Satan command the evil spirits to go directly to the Foot of the Cross[37] *to be judged and sentenced by Our Lord Jesus Christ – Amen.*

- When you feel the presence of evil around your surroundings, you should take authority in Jesus' name by rebuking the evil spirit verbally and with conviction. A prayer of rebuke can deliver you from obsessive disordered thoughts and fear which most likely have demonic origins. Our Blessed Lord used the prayer of rebuke in Matthew 4:10-11. He said: "'Get away, Satan!' It is written: 'The Lord, your God, shall you worship and him alone shall you serve.' Then the devil left him and, behold, angels came and ministered to him."

> *"When bad thoughts come you avert your mind's eye from them. Turn to the Lord and cast them out in his name"*[38]
>
> —St. Theophan the Recluse
> 19th century Russian spiritual master

Prayer of Rebuke
(2nd Sample prayer)

In the Name of Jesus, I rebuke the spirit of violence (or lust, or drunkenness, or mockery, or name of the vice) that is present at this place; evil spirit, I rebuke you, in Jesus Mighty Holy Precious name! Be gone to the foot of the cross, that Our Lord may do with you as He wills!

- Prayers of Rebuke are usually spontaneous prayer. The format is: 1) Rebuke the evil spirit 2) order it to leave your presence, 3) in Jesus name, power and authority.

3. Resist

Two key verses on Spiritual Warfare that give us answers and hope are:

> *"Be sober, be watchful. Your adversary the devil prowls around like a roaring lion, seeking someone to devour. Resist him, firm in your faith, knowing that the same experience of suffering is required of your brotherhood throughout the world."*
>
> —1 Peter 5:8-9

- Sobriety is the first and necessary step to protect yourself against the devil. A person who lives a life of intoxication is powerless against the devil. Intoxication destroys the budding seeds of the interior life.

  "...God opposes the proud, but gives grace to the humble. Submit yourselves therefore to God. Resist the devil and he will flee from you."

  —James 4:6-7

- Notice, we can resist the devil because we have free will.[39] We are not robots with a deterministic behavior that we have been programmed to follow.

After you 1) repent and 2) renounce, you still have to clean house. The devil is not going to simply walk out quietly. You are going to have to run him out in JESUS' name. The Bible says "Submit yourselves therefore to God. Resist the devil and he will flee from you." If you don't resist the devil, he is not going anywhere. If you try to resist the devil with unconfessed sin in your heart, he will laugh in your face and make a mockery of you. There must be 1) repentance, 2) renunciation and then there can be 3) resistance. Resistance against demonic attacks requires a strong sacramental life and prayer life which includes deliverance – healing prayers.

4. Renewal

Finally, we must be renewed in our spirit and in our mind. We must change our minds and think like Catholic Christians 24 hours a day, 7 days a week, 100% of the time.

> *"...and be renewed in the spirit of your minds, and put on the new nature, created after the likeness of God in true righteousness and holiness..."*
>
> —Ephesians 4:23-24

> *"Do not be conformed to this world but be transformed by the renewal of your mind, that you may prove what is the will of God, what is good and acceptable and perfect..."*
>
> —Romans 12:1-2

We all face a choice, we can walk away from God and serve the devil or we can be filled with the Holy Spirit and reject the devil. When the Bible says, "...be filled with the Spirit..." (Ephesians 5:18), this means that the Lord totally possesses our body and soul; there is not one room that HE doesn't have the key too.

1) Repent, 2) Renounce, 3) Resist and 4) Renew are steps to breaking Satan's stronghold in your life. Don't try to repent until you are honest and face your sin. Don't renounce until you have repented. Don't try to resist until you have repented and renounced. All these lead to a renewed mind, which means you have turned your back to Satan and to the glamor of evil, and now walk by the Holy Spirit. Here is the standard for all Christians.

> *"But I say, walk by the Spirit, and do not gratify the desires of the flesh. For the desires of the flesh are against the Spirit, and the desires of the Spirit are against the flesh; for these are opposed to each other, to prevent you from doing what you would...But the fruit of the Spirit is love, joy, peace, patience, kindness, goodness, faithfulness, gentleness, self-control; against such there is no law. And those who belong to Christ Jesus have crucified the flesh with its passions and desires. If we live by the Spirit, let us also walk by the Spirit."*
>
> —Galatians 5:16-17, 22-25

The Holy Spirit gives us the grace to walk in obedience. If one does not have internal law, one will never obey external law.

7 Steps to Freedom and Purity

1. **Abandon Your Will to God's Divine Will**

- Cry out for His help and trust only in His strength.
- It is only by humility and the grace of God that we can do this.
- Distrust yourself; you are your own worst enemy. Totally trust in JESUS.
- We are weak and too easily deceived by the lies of the enemy.
- You must want to abandon sin out of love for God. Remember the price He paid for your salvation – never forget the admonition: "how shall we escape if we neglect such a great a salvation" (Hebrews 2:3). *Yes, if we neglect the gospel we will not escape damnation.*

2. **Repent and Amend Your Life**

- Confess your sins to God in the Sacrament of Confession and confess your venial sins to the Lord every night and end with an "Act of Contrition."
- Strive daily for Interior Conversion.
- Avoid all occasions of Sin. Destroy all pornographic materials and access to porn. Put blockers on your Internet and TV Access.
- If you are Catholic, strive to learn your faith on a deeper level.

3. **Daily Prayer and Devotion**

- If you want to successfully overcome sins of the flesh and regain purity – prayer, meditation and devotion must play a central role in your struggle to strengthen your interior life.

- Read the Holy Bible every day.

- Pray the Holy Rosary daily.

- End every day by making a brief Examination of Conscience.

- Ask others to Intercede for you. Do not attempt this battle alone…ask your spouse, friends, family, accountability partner, pastor, a good confessor and don't forget to ask your Guardian Angel, and all the Angels and Saints to pray for you.

- Develop a healthy devotion to Sacramentals, they are a very powerful help to protect you in Spiritual Combat. These include: Holy Water, Crucifixes, Scapulars, Holy Medals, and Blessed Salt.

4. **Live a Sacramental Life**

- Go to regular Confession…at least monthly and as often as you fall into mortal sin.

- Attend Mass daily if possible, or visit Our Lord in the Blessed Sacrament daily if possible.

- Adoration of the Holy Eucharist at least once a week. Make time to stop by and visit Our Lord. For the benefits of Eucharistic Adoration (see page 154).

- If you are married, understand that your marriage is a Sacrament; which means we should try to lead our spouse to holiness daily.

5. **Consecrate Your Life to Christ and His Mother**

- Enthrone the Sacred Heart of Jesus in your home.
- Enroll yourself in the Brown Scapular of Our Lady of Mount Carmel.
- Consecrate yourself to Our Lady of the Miraculous Medal.

6. **Practice Fasting and Mortification**

- Fasting is powerful because it cleanses our soul and brings our flesh under control, this is called "self mastery." Through fasting we can strengthen the virtue of "temperance."
- It is a tool for obtaining a closer walk with God.
- It has the power to subdue the lower faculties of our flesh (sense appetites) and bring it under submission.
- If you are struggling with persistent sins, fasting is an effective way to help you break the enslavement to sins of the flesh.
- Fasting has stopped wars, healed the terminally ill, expelled demons and fasting with others is even more powerful.
- Humility, the one virtue that underlies every other virtue and conquers Satan's pride. Fasting defeats the devil, because it teaches how to rely on God and Control our passions. Humility + Fasting = two great weapons against Satan in the Spiritual Battle we face.

7. **Replace Vice with Virtue**

- The Practice of good Spiritual Exercises is indispensable in accomplishing this! Here are a few good books on Spiritual Exercises that have helped me. I recommend them to serious Catholics that want to be "Holy":

Imitation of Christ by Thomas Kempis

Spiritual Combat by Lorenzo Scupoli

Introduction to the Devout Life by Saint Francis de Sales

The Spiritual Exercises by St. Ignatius of Loyola

Clean of Heart: Overcoming Sins against Purity by Rosemarie Scott

The Official Book and Program of Healing of the Serenellians Apostolate – www.pornnomore.com

- Distractions – which may lead to Vice during your prayer time

  Voluntary distractions (cell phone, laptop, and television). You can do something about this.

  Involuntary distractions (uninvited bad thoughts). You must battle in choosing God over the uninvited thoughts. Don't give the thought any energy, discard the thought. St. Thomas More said: "Occupy your minds with good thoughts, or the enemy will fill them with bad ones. Unoccupied, they cannot be."

Demonic Thought Tampering

The following is the penetrating insight of a former Satanist on how demons tamper with our thoughts. She wrote a book: *A Message of Hope: Confessions of an Ex-Satanist* (Amor Deus Publishing) by Debra Lipsky.

How do demons afflict us? Through negative thoughts, says Lipsky. Through lying. Through anger. Through horror movies. Even a small leak in a boat can eventually sink it, she points out. "Demons 'feed' (figuratively) on negative thoughts which in turn excite them," she says. "Once you produce a negative thought, it has a frequency level that easily connects with a demon because like attracts like. This gives the demon access to your thoughts where he will plant similar thoughts so as to stay in your space. Isn't it amazing how one negative thought 'triggers' another and then another? Demons have an insatiable 'hunger' for negativity."

They (demons) also are attracted by "unresolved hurts" that fester over time like ugly wounds and "become like perfume that attracts demons." They love fear and anxiety because it gives them energy, and they hover around youngsters because teens are hormonally charged and prone to demonic lyrics that further rouse energy by evoking anger, defiance, lust, and rebellion. *Demons latch on to your thoughts through unconfessed sins.*

Also: "The quickest way a demon gains entrance is through occult involvement of any type," she writes. "It doesn't matter whether you practice black magic or just go to the latest three-d horror movie; both are an open invitation to demons that they don't refuse."

"Love is a powerful emotion, especially pure Godly love, which when demons are exposed to it, causes them to flee writhing in pain," notes (Debra) Lipsky. "Love torments a demon! Love reminds us that we are children of God and not slaves of the devil." [http://eucharistandmission.blogspot.com/2012/09/former-satanist-details-workings-of.html.]

12 Step Guide to Fighting Depression, Anxiety, and Stress

1. **Confession:** sacramental grace enables us to get rid of the cycle of guilt and sin in our lives.

2. **Forgiveness:** letting go of grudges, also forgiving yourself. Remember, "Anger" is one letter away from Danger. He who angers you, controls you!

3. **Acceptance of God's plan for our Lives:** accepting the reality of negative things in our life and the fact that this does not take away from God who has a beautiful plan and purpose for each one of us. Even the negative aspects in your life play a big role in this beautiful divine plan.

4. **Believing that God loves me:** God loves me with an everlasting unconditional love, even when I am depressed, He is with me.

5. **Gratitude:** having a attitude of gratitude is the key to defeating pessimism. I tell people when I am asked "How you doing?" I say, "I'm too blessed to be stressed, too anointed to be disappointed and "if hope was money I'd be a millionaire." Or "If being happy were a crime, I would be in jail" or "If I were any better, I'd be twins."

6. **Prayer:** be in constant communication with God our Father who is the Divine Healer and our "Wonderful Counselor" (cf. Isaiah 9:6).

7. **Holy Eucharist:** receive holy communion as often as possible, Jesus is our source of healing, He is the

antidote against sin and the medicine of immortality.

8. **Community:** find brothers and sisters in Christ for encouragement, support and accountability.

9. **Service:** involve yourself in the spiritual and corporal works of mercy. This will help you fight against isolation and egocentric negativity.

10. **Integration of the 5 aspects of our being:** *Spiritual* (most important - live daily in the presence of God), *physical* (get exercise, eat right), *mental* (read and listen to the right things), *emotional* (guard your senses), and *social* (maintain good company). God created and loves every part of who we are and wants us to be whole. We can't neglect one aspect.

11. **Living in the present moment:** Don't dwell on the past and don't worry about the future. The past is history, the future is mystery, learn to live in the sacrament of the present moment.

12. **Measuring Up (not down):** Judging ourselves from God's mirror and not from the world's standards.

[These 12 points taken from Alicia Leyva M.A., MFTI; recorded CD set entitled: *Steps to Overcome Depression*, recorded by St Josephs Communications, 2007].

STRESS (Webster Dictionary): anxiety, burden, pressure, worry.

The Psalmist was stressed and depressed. His remedy was to HOPE in the LORD. Read Psalm 42:5-11.

> *"Remember that stress is not always a bad thing. The purpose of stress is to alert us and protect us from real or perceived dangers, which is important for survival. Stress can excite us, prompt us to act, and force us to*

> *use creative problem solving techniques. Stress becomes harmful when the symptoms of stress overwhelm us and prevent us from functioning, at which point stress can even harm our health."*[40]
>
> — Dr. Ron Holman

Who can free you from anxiety or stress? **JESUS CAN!** Here is what the Priest prays after the 'Our Father' during Holy Mass. The Priest says, "Deliver us, Lord, from every evil, and grant us peace in our day. In your mercy keep us from sin and protect us from all ANXIETY (STRESS) as we wait in joyful hope for the coming of our Savior, Jesus Christ." This prayer is borrowed from Jesus' words in John 17:15 where he says, "I do not ask that you take them out of the world but that you keep them from the evil one."

4 Ways to Relieve Stress

1. "One of the best ways to relieve symptoms of stress is by talking to friends and family about what is on your mind. So often, just talking about your stressors and your fears makes them feel much smaller and less significant than what you have been creating in your mind."[41]

2. "Deep breathing works great when you are in the middle of a chaotic stressful event and you need to calm yourself down. Deep breathing lowers cortisol levels that spike during times of stress. A few deep breaths are typically sufficient to help most people calm down."[42]

3. "Research has shown that meditation can ease stress and anxiety. There are many guided meditations. Be

aware of the process that you are performing and notice all of your senses that are involved. If you notice that your mind has wandered, gently pull your attention back to the present."[43]

4. "Rest and relaxation are important to overall health, especially in times of stress. As little as 15 minutes a day of engaging in an activity that calms you and makes you feel good is enough to make significant change in the quality of your life."[44]

All 4 of these techniques can be done in Eucharistic Adoration of the Blessed Sacrament.

The best way to find Peace when your Stressed out is run to JESUS in Adoration.

How to Relieve Sorrow and Sadness

St. Thomas Aquinas can offer us practical wisdom for dealing with troublesome passions, partly because he so well grasps the implications of the fact that we are ensouled, mind-body unities. In prescribing "the remedies of sorrow and pain," he notes that when we have experienced an evil in the form of a loss or a negative event of some kind, we can lessen our distress by 1) experiencing pleasures of some kind, 2) weeping, 3) experiencing the sympathy of friends, 4) contemplating the truth, and indeed, even by 5) sleep and baths! St. Thomas tells us that "pleasure is to sorrow, what, in bodies, repose is to weariness" – it helps to counteract it.

> He notes that when Augustine mourned the death of his friend, "in groans and in tears alone did he find some little refreshment." In weeping, our focus is moved from our self-enclosed thoughts toward outward actions. Also, because groans and tears are

fitting actions to that state of passion, they produce a kind of pleasure. The sympathy of friends also works in a twofold manner. First, since sorrow depresses and weighs us down, when friends share our sorrows, it is as if they share our burdens and lessen the weight. Further, a friend's condolences show his love for us, and this is a source of great pleasure. When we contemplate the "truth" we move from the realm of the passions to the realm of the intellectual soul. When we read in James 1:2 (RSV) "Count it all joy my brethren, when you meet various trials," we see how the contemplation of our future happiness with God can diminish any sorrow. So much for the soul. As to the body, Augustine wrote that "the bath had its name from the fact of its driving sadness from the mind." St Ambrose reported, "Sleep restored the tired limbs to labor, refreshes the weary mind, and banishes sorrow."

[All of the above paragraph was taken from the book: *The One Minute Aquinas* by Kevin Vost; Sophia Press, p.33.]

Healing Power Prayers

"…It has been said that it is not a disgrace to be wounded on the battlefield. It is only a disgrace to dessert and quit the battle. When we sin, we must hear the voice of God calling us to repentance and healing, so that we can continue the fight against evil. Scripture is very clear about how much God wants us to be healed…"

—Jesse Romero

"For I will restore health to you, and your wounds I will heal, says the LORD…"

—Jeremiah 30:17

"But he was wounded for our transgressions, he was bruised for our iniquities; upon him was the chastisement that made us whole, and with his stripes we are healed."

—Isaiah 53:5

"He heels the brokenhearted, and binds up their wounds."

—Psalm 147:3

"So if the Son makes you free, you will be free indeed."

—John 8:36

"Jesus Christ is the same yesterday and today and forever."

—Hebrew 13:8

According to *Guidelines of Prayer for Healing*, a booklet published by the Doctrinal Commission of the International Catholic Charismatic Renewal Services (ICCRS), there are 4 basic categories of healing, namely:

1. **Physical Healing** – the healing from physical sickness and disability.
2. **Psychological Healing** – the healing of the wounds to the human psyche, including emotional wounds.
3. **Spiritual Healing** – the "healing from sin" that restores a person to a relationship with God.
4. **Exorcism & Deliverance** – healing and liberation from demonic influence.

Prayer for Healing

Almighty and merciful Father, by the power of your command, drive away from me all forms of sickness and disease. Restore strength to my body and joy to my spirit, so that in my renewed health, I may bless and serve you, now and forevermore — Amen.

Healing Prayer of Surrender

Dear Lord Jesus, it is my will to surrender to you everything that I am and everything that I'm striving to be. I open the deepest recesses of my heart to you and invite your Holy Spirit to dwell inside of me. I offer you my life, heart, mind, body, soul, spirit, all my hopes, plans and dreams. I surrender to you my past, present and future problems, habits, character defects, attitudes, livelihood, resources, finances, medical coverage, occupation and all my relationships. I give you my health, disabilities, physical appearance, home, family, marriage, children, sexuality and friendships. I ask you to take Lordship over every aspect of my life. I surrender to you all my hurt, pain, worry, anxiety and fear, and I ask you to wash me clean. I release everything into your compassionate care. Please speak to me clearly, Lord. Open my ears to hear your voice. Open my heart to commune with you more deeply. I desperately need to feel your loving embrace. Shut the doors that need to be shut and open the doors that need to be opened. Set my feet upon the straight and narrow road that leads to everlasting life — Amen.

Prayer for Family's of Persons in Need of Healing / Intervention

Heavenly Father, protect them and their house from all evils and misfortunes, grant that they may be ever resigned to Thy divine will even in the sorrows which it shall please Thee to send them. Finally, give unto all of us the grace to live in perfect harmony and in the fullness of love toward our neighbor. Grant that every one of us may deserve by a holy life the comfort of Thy holy Sacraments at the hour of death. O Jesus, bless them and protect them — Amen.

Prayer for Inner Healing

Dear Lord Jesus, please come and heal my wounded and troubled heart. I beg you to heal the torments that are causing anxiety in my life. I beg you, in a particular way, to heal the underlying source of my sinfulness. I beg you to come into my life and heal the psychological harms that struck me in my childhood and from the injuries that have caused emotional pain throughout my life.

Lord Jesus, you know my burdens. I lay them on your Good

Shepherd's Heart. I beseech you by the merits of the great open wound in your heart, to heal the small wounds that are in mine. Heal my memories, so that nothing that has happened to me will cause me to remain in pain and anguish, filled with anxiety.

Heal, O Lord, all those wounds that have been the cause of all the evil that is rooted in my life. I want to forgive all those who have offended me. Look to those inner sores that make me unable to forgive. You who came to forgive the afflicted of heart, please heal my wounded and troubled heart.

Heal, O Lord Jesus, all those intimate wounds that cause me physical illness. I offer you my heart. Accept it, Lord, purify it and give me the sentiments of your Divine Heart.

Heal me, O Lord, from the pain caused by the death of my loved ones. Grant me to regain peace and joy in the knowledge that you are the Resurrection and the Life. Make me an authentic witness to your resurrection, your victory over sin and death, and your loving presence among all men — Amen.

Prayer of Reconciliation

Dear Lord Jesus, for the sake of your sorrowful passion, I ask you to forgive all my sins, especially those that have allowed any form of sickness or disease to enter my body and harm my health. I humbly ask you to send forth the Holy Spirit's gift of conviction and shine the light of truth into the deepest recesses of my soul, so that I may make a complete act of contrition before you now.

Lord Jesus, please forgive me for all my sins, especially for any unknown and hidden sins. I am heartily sorry for having offended you. I ask forgiveness for all the times I failed to make you Lord over my life. Forgive me for having other gods before you; for making idols out of created things and serving them; for taking your most holy name in vain and for failing to observe the Sabbath day of rest. Please forgive me for not honoring my father and mother, committing the sin of adultery or abortion, stealing, bearing false witness and coveting my neighbor's spouse, property and possessions.

Please forgive me for not loving You with my whole heart, mind, soul and strength, for not loving my neighbor as myself and for disrespecting the temple of your Holy Spirit. Please forgive me for not taking better care of my health, for eating unhealthy foods and poisoning my body with chemicals, drugs, alcohol, nicotine and any other harmful substance or medication.

Please forgive me for committing the sins of hypocrisy, intolerance, unforgiveness, ungratefulness, disbelief, deception, disobedience, envy, pride, fantasy, fornication, idolatry, impatience, division, dissension, offending others, hard-heartedness, hate, haughtiness, anger, rebellion, gambling, greed, intimidation, jealousy, perfectionism, judgmentalness, lust, legalism, manipulation, resentment, rudeness, sexual idolatry, sexual immorality, sexual impurity, sexual perversion, selfishness, self-centeredness, self-righteousness, self-pity, slander, worry, vanity, worldliness, witchcraft, addictions, dependencies, complaining, gossiping and all other forms of unrighteousness.

Lord Jesus, I ask you to forgive me for all my sins, trespasses and transgressions and to cover all my offenses with your most precious blood. Surround me with your light and penetrate the very depths of my being with your love. Let no area of darkness remain in me, but transform my whole being with the healing light of your infinite love — Amen.

God's healing Love

In the name of Jesus I pray that you release your healing love into my body, mind and soul. I thank you and praise you Lord Jesus Christ — Amen.

To Claim Someone to Christ

Heavenly Father, I ask You in the name of Jesus, and through the precious blood of Jesus Christ to rebuke Satan for taking captive that which is your creation. And I ask You Lord Jesus, to place your crown of thorns around [name] and draw [him/her] to Your Sacred Heart under your mantle of Love. Mother Mary most Holy, please hold [name] in the mantle of your motherly protection and cover [name] with the veil of your holiness — Amen.

Prayer for a Person with Addictions

Lord Jesus, You said, "I have come to set the captives free." This person is captive and needs your healing touch to be set free. Lord, please free [name] from their addiction, so that [he/she] will be free from the cares and worries that prevent [his/her] happiness and holiness; free [name] from those sins that cling to [him/her], and to those sins which [he/she] clings too; free [name] from all compulsive behavior that prevents [him/her] from becoming your holy child. Bring your child, loving Savior, to the experience of the abundant life which you promised — Amen.

Prayer for a Creative Miracle

God of all creation, you who spoke a simple command and brought forth light from the darkness, I call upon you now to send forth your miracle-working power into every aspect of my being. In the same way that you spoke unto the dust of the ground when you created humankind in your own image, I ask you to send forth your healing power into my body. Send forth your word and command every cell, electrical and chemical impulse, tissue, joint, ligament, organ, gland, muscle, bone and every molecule in my body to come under complete and perfect health, strength, alignment, balance and harmony.

It is through you that I live and move and have my being. With every breath I take, I live under your life-giving grace. I ask you to touch me now with the same miracle-working power that you used when you fashioned me inside my mother's womb. As surely as you have created me in your image and likeness, you can also recreate me now and restore me to health.

Please fill me with your healing power. Cast out all that should not be inside of me right now. I ask you to mend all that is broken, root out every sickness and disease, open all blocked arteries and veins, restore my internal organs, rebuild my damaged tissues, remove all inflammation and cleanse me of all infections, viruses and destructive forms of bacteria.

Let the warmth of your healing love flood my entire being, so that my body will function the way it was created to be, whole and complete, renewed in your perfect health. I ask this through my Lord, Jesus Christ, your Son, who lives and reigns with you and the Holy Spirit, one God, for ever and ever — Amen.

Prayer for Peaceful Rest

Dear Lord Jesus, as I rest in the comfort of your love, I ask to experience your gentle embrace as you tenderly wrap your loving arms around me. I trust your compassionate care will bring peace to my mind, serenity to my heart and renewal to my spirit.

In your loving embrace, I ask that you grant me a peaceful night's rest. Please purify my dreams, cleanse my subconscious and wash my thoughts with the purity of your infinite love. Please minister to my heart, mind, body and soul as I rest in your compassionate care tonight.

Please send forth your protective angels to stand guard over me as I sleep. May your angelic army destroy all curses, hindrances and demonic influences that have been sent against my ability to experience a peaceful night's rest. I ask that your heavenly host protect me as I stay awake and watch over me as I sleep, that awake I may keep watch with Christ, and asleep, rest in his peace — Amen

Serenity Prayer

(A perfect prayer for stress)

God, grant me the serenity to accept the things I cannot change; courage to change the things I can; and the wisdom to know the difference. Living one day at a time; accepting hardships as the pathway to peace; taking as He did, this sinful world as it is, not as I would have it; trusting that He will make all things right if I surrender to His will; that I may be reasonably happy in this life and supremely happy with Him forever in the next. —Amen.

'Let us flee, for she is not alone; the Almighty is with her!' And they vanished like dust, like the noise of the road, while I continued on my way to my cell undisturbed, finishing my 'Te Deum' and pondering the infinite and unfathomable mercy of God."

— St. Faustina Kowalska (paragraph 320)

"Christians are, moreover, born for combat"

—Pope Leo XIII (*Sapientiae Christianae*)

"There is a battle for souls mentioned in Ephesians 6. All of humanity is under attack. When we sin, we cooperate with evil. This makes us vulnerable to the attacks of Devil in even more serious ways. When trying to fight against the Enemy, the Sacrament of Reconciliation and Holy Communion are very powerful, they are like a heavyweight boxing Champion's one - two punch. We must keep fighting by our prayers and fasting until we here the last trumpet sound. Here are some additional prayers that I have found to be most effective in the battle against the Enemy..."

—Jesse Romero

Prayer for Putting on The Armor of God

That I may be able to stand firm against the tactics of the devil, I now put on the whole Armor of God.

I put on the helmet of Salvation. Lord Jesus, You are my Salvation.

I put on the breastplate of Righteousness, and the belt of Truth. Lord Jesus, You are my Righteousness, and my Truth.

I put on the shoes for spreading the Gospel of Peace. Lord Jesus, You are my Peace.

I carry the shield of Faith and the sword of the Spirit, the Word of God. Lord Jesus, You are my Faith! You are the Living Word. And in You, O Lord, I place all my trust — Amen.

St. Michael Prayer

St. Michael the Archangel, defend us in battle. Be our defense against the wickedness and snares of the devil. May God rebuke him we humbly pray and do thou, O Prince of the heavenly host, by the power of God, cast into Hell Satan and all the evil spirits who prowl about the world seeking the ruin of souls — Amen.

Exorcism Prayer by St. Anthony

Behold the Cross of the Lord! Begone, all evil powers! The Lion of the tribe of Judah, the Root of David, has conquered! Alleluia, Alleluia!
[Pope Sixtus V engraved this prayer on the base of the obelisk at St. Peter's Square]

Prayer Against Evil

In the name of the Father, Son and Holy Spirit, Most Holy Trinity, descend upon me. Please purify me, mold me, fill me with yourself, and use me. Banish from me all spells, witchcraft, black magic, demonic assignments, malefice, maledictions and the evil eye; diabolic infestations, oppressions, possessions; all that is evil and sinful; jealousy, treachery, envy; all physical, psychological, moral, and spiritual attacks against me. Banish all the forces of evil from me; destroy them, vanquish them so that I can be healthy and do good deeds. Banish all diabolical ailments; as well as all enticing spirits, deaf, dumb, blind, mute and sleeping spirits, new-age spirits, occult spirits, religious spirits, antichrist spirits, and any other spirits of death and darkness. I command and bid all the powers who molest me—by the power of God Almighty, in the name of Jesus Christ our Savior—to leave me forever, and to be consigned into the everlasting lake of fire, that they may never again touch me or any other creature in the entire world — Amen.

Renouncing the Occult

Heavenly Father, in the name of your only begotten Son, Jesus Christ, I renounce Satan and all his works, all forms of witchcraft, the use of divination, the practice of sorcery, dealing with mediums, channeling with spirit guides, the Ouija board, astrology, Reiki, hypnosis, automatic writing, horoscopes, numerology, all types of fortune telling, palm readings, levitation, and anything else associated with the occult or Satan. I renounce all of them in the name of Jesus Christ who came in the flesh, and by the power of his cross, his blood and his resurrection, I break their hold over my life.

I confess all these sins before you and ask you to cleanse and forgive me. I ask you Lord Jesus to enter my heart and create in me the kind of person you have intended me to be. I ask you to send forth the gifts of your Holy Spirit to baptize me, just as you baptized your disciples on the day of Pentecost.

I thank you heavenly Father for strengthening my inner spirit with the power of your Holy Spirit, so that Christ may dwell in my heart. Through faith, rooted and grounded in love, may I be able to comprehend with all the saints, the breadth, length, height and depth of Christ's love which surpasses all knowledge — Amen.

Destroying Demonic Influence

Through the power of our Lord Jesus Christ of Nazareth, I come against every source of sin in my life. I ask you Lord Jesus to send forth an assignment of warring angels to strike down and destroy every demonic entity that has been influencing my sinful behaviors of envy, criticism, impatience, resentment, pride, rebellion, stubbornness, unforgiveness, gossip, disobedience, strife, violence, divorce, accusation, anger, manipulation, jealousy, greed, laziness, revenge, coveting, possessiveness, control, retaliation, selfishness, deceitfulness, deception, dishonesty, unbelief, seduction, lust, pornography, masturbation, idolatry and witchcraft.

May your warring angels strike down and destroy every demonic influence that has contributed to my physical and psychological infirmities of nerve disorder, lung disorder, brain disorder or dysfunction, AIDS, cancer, hypochondria, hyperactivity, depression, schizophrenia, fatigue, anorexia, bulimia, addictions, gluttony, perfectionism, alcoholism, self-abuse, sexual addictions, sexual perversions, attempted suicide, incest, pedophilia, lesbianism, homosexuality, adultery, homophobia, confusion, ignorance, procrastination, self-hatred, isolation, loneliness, ostracism, paranoia, nervousness, passivity, indecision, doubt, oppression, rejection, poor self-image, anxiety, shame, timidity and fear.

I arise today through the power of the Lord Jesus Christ and ask to be filled with the Holy Spirit's gifts of peace, patience, love, joy, kindness, generosity, faithfulness, gentleness, self-control, humility, forgiveness, goodness, fortitude, discipline, truth, relinquishment, good self-image, prosperity, charity, obedience, a sound mind, order, fulfillment in Christ, acceptance of self, acceptance of others, trust, freedom from addictions, freedom of having-to-control, freedom from shame, wholeness, wellness, health, wisdom, knowledge, understanding, and the light and life of the Lord Jesus Christ — Amen.

Prayer for a Spiritual Canopy

Dear Lord Jesus, please forgive me for all the times I have not submitted to your will in my life. Please forgive me for all my sinful actions, making agreements with the enemy, and for believing the devil's lies. I now submit to you as my Lord, dear Jesus. Now I break every agreement that I have made with the enemy.

Lord Jesus, please have your warring angels remove and bind to the abyss all demons and their devices that had access to me because I believed their lies. Lord Jesus Christ, I now ask you to establish a hedge of protection around me, over me and under me, and seal it with your blood.

I now choose to put on the full armor of God and ask that you cleanse me and seal me, body, mind and soul with your blood, Lord Jesus Christ. Please have your warring angels bind up and remove all demons, their devices, and all their power from within this protective hedge and have them sent to the abyss.

Please have your warrior angels destroy all demonic, occult or witchcraft assignments directed against me including all backups and replacements. Please have your angels stand guard over me and protect me from all the attacks of the enemy — Amen.

Prayer against Malefice

Holy God, our Lord, King of ages, All-powerful and Almighty, you who made everything and who transform everything simply by your will; you who changed into dew the flames of the seven-times hotter furnace and protected and saved your three holy children:

You are the doctor and physician of my soul. You are the salvation of those who turn to you. I beseech you to make powerless, banish, and drive out every diabolic power, presence and machination; every evil influence, malefice or evil eye and all evil actions aimed against me.

Where there is envy and malice, give me an abundance of goodness, endurance, victory and charity. O Lord, you who love man, I beg you to reach out your powerful holy hands and your most high and mighty arms and come to my aid.

Send your angel of peace over me, to protect my body and soul. May he keep at bay and vanquish every evil power, every poison or malice invoked against me by corrupt and envious people.

Then under the protection of your authority may I sing with gratitude, "The Lord is my salvation; whom should I fear?" I will not fear evil because you are with me, my God, my strength, my powerful Lord, King of peace, Father of all ages — Amen.

Healing the Family Tree

Heavenly Father, I come before you as your child, in great need of your help; I have physical health needs, emotional needs, spiritual needs and interpersonal needs. Many of my problems have been caused by my own failures, neglect and sinfulness, for which I humbly beg your forgiveness, Lord. But I also ask you to forgive the sins of my ancestors whose failures have left their effects on me in the form of unwanted tendencies, behavior patterns, and defects in body, mind and spirit. Heal me, Lord, from all these disorders.

With your help I sincerely forgive everyone, living or dead members of my family tree, who have directly offended me or my loved ones in any way, or those whose sins have resulted in our present sufferings and disorders. In the name of your divine Son Jesus, and in the power of the Holy Spirit, I ask you Father, to deliver me and my entire family tree from the influence of the evil one.

Free all living and dead members of my family tree, including those in adoptive relationships, and those in extended family relationships from every contaminating form of bondage. By your loving concern for us, heavenly Father, and by the shed blood of your precious Son Jesus, I beg you to extend your blessing to me and all my living and deceased relatives. Heal every negative effect transmitted through all past generations, and prevent such negative effects in future generations of my family tree.

I symbolically place the cross of Jesus over the head of each person in my family tree, and between each generation; I ask you to let the cleansing blood of Jesus purify the bloodlines in my family lineage. Send protective angels to encamp around us and administer your divine healing power to all of us. Give special power to our family members' guardian angels to heal, protect, guide and encourage each of us in all our needs. Let your healing power be released at this very moment, and let it continue as long as your sovereignty permits.

In our family tree, Lord, replace all bondage to sin with a holy bonding of family love and let there be an ever-deeper bonding with you, Lord. Let the family of the Holy Trinity pervade my family with its tender, warm, loving presence, so that our family may recognize and manifest that love in all our relationships. All of my unknown needs that will make me holier I include with this petition. This we pray in Jesus' precious name through Mary's intercession — Amen.

Psalm 91

You who live in the shelter of the Most High, who abide in the shadow of the Almighty, will say to the Lord, "My refuge and my fortress; my God, in whom I trust." For he will deliver you from the snare of the fowler and from the deadly pestilence; he will cover you with his pinions, and under his wings you will find refuge; his faithfulness is a shield and buckler.

You will not fear the terror of the night, or the arrow that flies by day, or the pestilence that stalks in darkness, or the destruction that wastes at noonday. A thousand may fall at your side, ten thousand at your right hand, but it will not come near you. You will only look with your eyes and see the punishment of the wicked. Because you have made the Lord your refuge, the Most High your dwelling place, no evil shall befall you, no scourge come near your tent.

For he will command his angels concerning you to guard you in all your ways. On their hands they will bear you up, so that you will not dash your foot against a stone. You will tread on the lion and the adder, the young lion and the serpent you will trample under foot. Those who love me, I will deliver; I will protect those who know my name. When they call to me, I will answer them; I will be with them in trouble, I will rescue them and honor them. With long life I will satisfy them, and show them my salvation — Amen.

Pleading the Blood of Jesus

Father in Heaven, may we all be cleansed by the saving Blood of Jesus; may our consciences be purged of dead works.

For Salvation, that none of us would be lost, led astray or deceived, we plead the Precious Blood of Jesus.

For Safety, that we would all be protected and safe from all spiritual, mental, and physical harm, we plead the Precious Blood of Jesus.

For Ministry, that I may fulfill the duties of my apostolate like a faithful soldier of Christ, we plead the Precious Blood of Jesus.

For Marriage, that God would heal the things that are wounded or broken in my marriage and strengthen what is good, we plead the Precious Blood of Jesus.

For Our Children, that God would protect them from physical and spiritual harm and lead them in His paths. That they not stray from the faith and for our sake as parents, to raise them to know the Lord, we plead the Precious Blood of Jesus.

For Our Relationships, that all of our relationships would be based on good, holy and Godly principles, we plead the Precious Blood of Jesus.

For Our Health, that we would all be made whole, spiritually, mentally and physically, we plead the Precious Blood of Jesus.

For Our Homes, that they would be protected from destruction, spiritually, physically, or materially. That they would be havens from the world for us and places where God's love is shared, we plead the Precious Blood of Jesus.

For Our Vehicles, that we would be protected in all of our travels. Keep us safe from accidents or harm, that no one may ever be injured through them; we plead the Precious Blood of Jesus.

For Our Finances, that God would bless our jobs, businesses, and that our needs would be met, we plead the Precious Blood of Jesus.

We mark the borders of our nation and the door posts of our churches, homes, schools and places of employment with the Precious Blood of Jesus. We thank You, Lord, for shedding Your Blood for us. May the Blood and Water that came from the side of Jesus, create a protecting fountain of grace, one which flows directly from the throne of God to us. Come, Lord, and fill us with Your Holy Spirit — Amen.

Offering of the Precious Blood / Closing of Deliverance Prayers

Eternal Father, I offer You the Most Precious Blood of Jesus Christ in atonement for my sins, and in supplication for the holy souls in Purgatory and for the needs of Holy Mother Church. Thank you Lord Jesus for opening my spiritual eyes and bringing me into your light. Thank you Lord, for transforming me by the renewing of my mind. Thank you Lord, for pouring out your Spirit on me, and revealing your Word to me. Thank you Lord, for giving your angels charge over me in all my ways. Thank you for the gift of my Catholic faith, I beg you Lord, that from my innermost being shall flow rivers of living water. Thank you for directing my mind and heart to the Sacred Heart of Jesus and the Immaculate Heart of Mary. Fill me to overflowing with your life and love, my blessed Lord and King Jesus Christ — Amen.

A Prayer for Protection

(to be prayed before ministry of healing and deliverance)

In the name of Jesus Christ and by the power of his Cross and his blood, we bind up the power of any evil spirits and command them not to block our prayers. We bind up the powers of earth, air, water, fire, the netherworld and the satanic forces of nature. We break any curses, hexes or spells sent against us and declare them null and void. We break the assignments of any spirits sent against us and send them to Jesus to deal with them as he wills. Lord, we ask you to bless our enemies by sending your Holy Spirit to lead them to repentance and conversion. Furthermore, we bind any and all interaction in the world of evil spirits as it affects us and our ministry.

We ask for the protection of the shed blood of Jesus Christ over ___________. Thank you, Lord, for your protection and send your angels, especially St. Michael, the Archangel, to help us in the battle. We ask you to guide us in our prayers: share with us your Spirit's power and compassion —Amen. (By Dr. Francis MacNutt).

Prayer to be Set Free

(to be prayed following ministry of Deliverance)

Lord Jesus, thank you for sharing with us your wonderful ministry of healing and deliverance. Thank you for the healings we have seen and experienced today. We realize that the sickness and evil we encounter is more than our humanity can bear, so cleanse us of any sadness, negativity or despair that we may have picked up. If our ministry has tempted us to anger, impatience or lust, cleanse us of those temptations and replace them with love, joy and peace.

If any evil spirits have attached themselves to us or oppressed us in any way, we command you, spirits of earth, air, fire or water, or the netherworld or of nature, to depart — now — and go straight to Jesus Christ for him to deal with you as he wills.

Come Holy Spirit: renew us – fill us anew with your power, your life and your joy. Strengthen us where we have felt weak and clothe us with your light. Fill us with life. Lord Jesus, please send your holy angels to minister to our families – guard us and protect us from all sickness, harm and accidents. (Give us a safe trip home).

We praise you now and forever, Father, Son, and Holy Spirit, and we ask these things in Jesus Holy Name that He may be glorified — Amen. (By Dr. Francis MacNutt)

Make war on the floor, get on your knees and pray. Satan trembles when the weakest saint gets down on their knees.

Auxilium Christianorum Prayers

(Help of Christians)

These prayers were compiled and written by a team of Exorcist for use by the laity for themselves and their loved ones to be healed and protected from the demonic.

www.auxiliumchristianorum.org

1. Prayers to Be Said Everyday:

V. Our help is in the name of the Lord.
R. Who made Heaven and Earth.

Most gracious Virgin Mary, thou who wouldst crush the head of the serpent, protect us from the vengeance of the evil one. We offer our prayers, supplications, sufferings and good works to thee so that thou may purify them, sanctify them and present them to thy Son as a perfect offering. May this offering be given so that the demons that influence or seek to influence the members of the Auxilium Christianorum do not know the source of their expulsion and blindness. Blind them so that they know not our good works. Blind them so that they know not on whom to take vengeance. Blind them so that they may receive the just sentence for their works. Cover us with the Precious Blood of thy Son so that we may enjoy the protection which flows from His Passion and Death. We ask this through the same Christ our Lord — Amen.

St. Michael Prayer (See pages 51, 58, and 106)

Guardian Angel Prayer (See pages 51 and 58)

Our Father (See page 49)

Hail Mary (See pages 18 and 50)

Glory Be (See page 52)

2. Litany of the Most Precious Blood of Our Lord Jesus Christ:

V. Lord have mercy.
R. Lord have mercy

V. Christ have mercy.
R. Christ have mercy

V. Lord have mercy.
R. Lord have mercy

V. Christ hear us.
R. Christ graciously hear us.

God the Father of Heaven, have mercy on us.
God the Son, Redeemer of the world, have mercy on us.
God the Holy Spirit, have mercy on us.
Holy Trinity, One God, have mercy on us.

Blood of Christ, only-begotten Son of the Eternal Father, save us.
Blood of Christ, Incarnate Word of God, save us.
Blood of Christ, of the New and Eternal Testament, save us.
Blood of Christ, falling upon the Earth in the Agony, save us.
Blood of Christ, shed profusely in the Scourging, save us.
Blood of Christ, flowing forth in the Crowning with Thorns, save us.
Blood of Christ, poured out on the Cross, save us.
Blood of Christ, price of our salvation, save us.
Blood of Christ, without which there is no forgiveness, save us.
Blood of Christ, Eucharistic drink and refreshment of souls, save us.
Blood of Christ, stream of mercy, save us.

Blood of Christ, victor over demons, save us.
Blood of Christ, courage of Martyrs, save us.
Blood of Christ, strength of Confessors, save us.
Blood of Christ, bringing forth Virgins, save us.
Blood of Christ, help of those in peril, save us.
Blood of Christ, relief of the burdened, save us.
Blood of Christ, solace in sorrow, save us.
Blood of Christ, hope of the penitent, save us.
Blood of Christ, consolation of the dying, save us.
Blood of Christ, peace and tenderness of hearts, save us.
Blood of Christ, pledge of eternal life, save us.
Blood of Christ, freeing souls from purgatory, save us.
Blood of Christ, most worthy of all glory and honor, save us.

Lamb of God, Who taketh away the sins of the world, spare us, O Lord.
Lamb of God, Who taketh away the sins of the world, graciously hear us, O Lord.
Lamb of God, Who taketh away the sins of the world, have mercy on us.

V. Thou hast redeemed us with Thy Blood, O Lord.
R. And made of us a kingdom for our God.

Let us pray: Almighty, and everlasting God, Who hast appointed Thine only-begotten Son to be the Redeemer of the world, and hast been pleased to be reconciled unto us by His Blood, grant us, we beseech Thee, so to venerate with solemn worship the price of our salvation, that the power thereof may here on Earth keep us from all things hurtful, and the fruit of the same may gladden us forever hereafter in Heaven. Through the same Christ our Lord.
R. Amen.

3. On Sundays:

O Glorious Queen of Heaven and Earth, Virgin Most Powerful, thou who hast the power to crush the head of the ancient serpent with thy heel, come and exercise this power flowing from the grace of thine Immaculate Conception. Shield us under the mantle of thy purity and love, draw us into the sweet abode of thy heart and annihilate and render impotent the forces bent on destroying us. Come Most Sovereign Mistress of the Holy Angels and Mistress of the Most Holy Rosary, thou who from the very beginning hast received from God the power and the mission to crush the head of Satan. Send forth thy holy legions, we humbly beseech thee, that under thy command and by thy power they may pursue the evil spirits, counter them on every side, resist their bold attacks and drive them far from us, harming no one on the way, binding them to the foot of the Cross to be judged and sentenced by Jesus Christ Thy Son and to be disposed of by Him as He wills. St. Joseph, Patron of the Universal Church, come to our aid in this grave battle against the forces of darkness, repel the attacks of the devil and free the members of the Auxilium Christianorum, and those for whom the priests of the Auxilium Christianorum pray, from the strongholds of the enemy. St. Michael, summon the entire heavenly court to engage their forces in this fierce battle against the powers of Hell. Come O Prince of Heaven with thy mighty sword and thrust into Hell Satan and all the other evil spirits. O Guardian Angels, guide and protect us —Amen.

4. On Mondays:

In Thy name, Lord Jesus Christ, we pray that Thou cover us, our families, and all of our possessions with Thy love and Thy Most Precious Blood and surround us with Thy Heavenly Angels, Thy Saints and the mantle of Our Blessed Mother — Amen.

5. On Tuesdays:

Lord Jesus Christ, we beg Thee for the grace to remain guarded beneath the protective mantle of Mary, surrounded by the holy briar from which was taken the Holy Crown of Thorns, and saturated with Thy Precious Blood in the power of the Holy Spirit, with our Guardian Angels, for the greater glory of the Father — Amen.

6. On Wednesdays:

In the Name of Jesus Christ, Our Lord and God, we ask Thee to render all spirits impotent, paralyzed and ineffective in attempting to take revenge against anyone of the members of the Auxilium Christianorum, our families, friends, communities, those who pray for us and their family members, or anyone associated with us and for whom the priests of the Auxilium Christianorum pray. We ask Thee to bind all evil spirits, all powers in the air, the water, the ground, the fire, underground, or wherever they exercise their powers, any satanic forces in nature and any and all emissaries of the satanic headquarters. We ask Thee to bind by Thy Precious Blood all of the attributes, aspects and characteristics, interactions, communications and deceitful games of the evil spirits. We ask Thee to break any and all bonds, ties and attachments in the Name of the Father, and of the Son and of the Holy Spirit — Amen.

7. On Thursdays:

My Lord, Thou art all powerful, Thou art God, Thou art our Father. We beg Thee through the intercession and help of the Archangels St. Michael, Raphael, and Gabriel for the deliverance of our brothers and sisters who are enslaved by the evil one. All Saints of Heaven, come to our aid.

- From anxiety, sadness and obsessions – We implore Thee, deliver us, O Lord.
- From hatred, fornication, and envy – We implore Thee, deliver us, O Lord.

- From thoughts of jealousy, rage, and death – We implore Thee, deliver us, O Lord.
- From every thought of suicide and abortion – We implore Thee, deliver us, O Lord.
- From every form of sinful sexuality – We implore Thee, deliver us, O Lord.
- From every division in our family, and every harmful friendship – We implore Thee, deliver us, O Lord.
- From every sort of spell, malefice, witchcraft, and every form of the occult – We implore Thee, deliver us, O Lord.

Thou who said, "Peace I leave with you, my peace I give unto you." Grant that, through the intercession of the Virgin Mary, we may be liberated from every demonic influence and enjoy Thy peace always, In the Name of Christ, our Lord — Amen.

8. On Fridays:

Litany of Humility

"When pride comes, disgrace comes;
but with the humble is wisdom."

—Proverbs 11:2

"Learn of Me, because I am meek and Humble of Heart."

—Jesus Christ (Mt. 11:29)

O Jesus, meek and humble of heart, hear me.
From the desire of being esteemed, deliver me Jesus.

From the desire of being loved, deliver me Jesus.
From the desire of being extolled, deliver me Jesus.
From the desire of being honored, deliver me Jesus.
From the desire of being praised, deliver me Jesus.
From the desire of being preferred to others, deliver me Jesus.
From the desire of being consulted, deliver me Jesus.
From the desire of being approved, deliver me Jesus.
From the fear of being humiliated, deliver me Jesus.
From the fear of being despised, deliver me Jesus.
From the fear of suffering rebukes, deliver me Jesus.
From the fear of being calumniated, deliver me Jesus.
From the fear of being forgotten, deliver me Jesus.
From the fear of being ridiculed, deliver me Jesus.
From the fear of being wronged, deliver me Jesus.
From the fear of being suspected, deliver me Jesus.

That others may be loved more than I, Jesus, grant me the grace to desire it.
That others may be esteemed more than I, Jesus, grant me the grace to desire it.
That in the opinion of the world, others may increase and I may decrease, Jesus, grant me the grace to desire it.
That others may be chosen and I set aside, Jesus, grant me the grace to desire it.
That others may be praised and I unnoticed, Jesus, grant me the grace to desire it.
That others may be preferred to me in everything, Jesus, grant me the grace to desire it.
That others may become holier than I, provided that I become as holy as I should, Jesus, grant me the grace to desire it — Amen.

9. On Saturdays:

O God and Father of our Lord Jesus Christ, we call upon Thy holy Name and humbly beseech Thy clemency, that, through the intercession of the ever Immaculate Virgin, our Mother Mary, and of the glorious Archangel Saint Michael, thou wouldst vouchsafe to help us against Satan and all the other unclean spirits that are prowling about the world to the great peril of the human race and the loss of souls — Amen.

10. Conclusion for Every Day:

August Queen of the Heavens, heavenly Sovereign of the Angels, Thou who from the beginning hast received from God the power and the mission to crush the head of Satan, we humbly beseech Thee to send thy holy legions, so that under Thy command and through Thy power, they may pursue the demons and combat them everywhere, suppress their boldness, and drive them back into the abyss. O good and tender Mother, Thou wilt always be our love and hope! O Divine Mother, send Thy Holy Angels to defend us and to drive far away from us the cruel enemy. Holy Angels and Archangels defend us, guard us — Amen.

Most Sacred Heart of Jesus, have mercy on us.
Mary, Help of Christians, pray for us.
Virgin Most Powerful, pray for us.
St. Joseph terror of demons, pray for us.
St. Michael the Archangel, pray for us.

All You Holy Angels and Saints pray for us.

We cover ourselves with the precious blood of Jesus and put on the full armor of God, in the name of the Father, the Son and the Holy Spirit — Amen.

Final Miscellaneous Prayers

The Universal Prayer

(Attributed to Pope Clement XI)

Lord, I believe in you: increase my faith.
I trust in you: strengthen my trust.
I love you: let me love you more and more.
I am sorry for my sins: deepen my sorrow.

I worship you as my first beginning,
I long for you as my last end,
I praise you as my constant helper,
And call on you as my loving protector.

Guide me by your wisdom,
Correct me with your justice,
Comfort me with your mercy,
Protect me with your power.

I offer you, Lord, my thoughts: to be fixed on you;
My words: to have you for their theme;
My actions: to reflect my love for you;
My sufferings: to be endured for your greater glory.

I want to do what you ask of me:
In the way you ask,
For as long as you ask,
Because you ask it.

Lord, enlighten my understanding,
Strengthen my will,
Purify my heart,

And make me holy.

Help me to repent of my past sins
And to resist temptation in the future.
Help me to rise above my human weaknesses
And to grow stronger as a Christian.

Let me love you, my Lord and my God,
And see myself as I really am:
A pilgrim in this world,
A Christian called to respect and love
All whose lives I touch,
Those under my authority,
My friends and my enemies.

Help me to conquer anger with gentleness,
Greed by generosity,
Apathy by fervor.
Help me to forget myself
And reach out toward others.

Make me prudent in planning,
Courageous in taking risks.
Make me patient in suffering, unassuming in prosperity.

Keep me, Lord, attentive at prayer,
Temperate in food and drink,
Diligent in my work,
Firm in my good intentions.

Let my conscience be clear,
My conduct without fault,
My speech blameless,
My life well-ordered.
Put me on guard against my human weaknesses.
Let me cherish your love for me,
Keep your law,
And come at last to your salvation.

Teach me to realize that this world is passing,
That my true future is the happiness of Heaven,
That life on Earth is short,
And the life to come eternal.

Help me to prepare for death
With a proper fear of judgment,
But a greater trust in your goodness.
Lead me safely through death
To the endless joy of Heaven.

Grant this through Christ our Lord — Amen.

Prayer for the Heart

"Do you know what the most beautiful moment of the day is? It is when you pray, because you speak with the One Who loves you most."

—Anonymous

Please take a moment to relax your mind and humble your heart to focus on Christ. Allow God to be the only person on your mind while you read this prayer. If we can take the time to read long jokes, stories, etc., we should give the same respect to this prayer. Friends and family who pray together, stay together.

Dear Lord, I thank you for this day. I thank You for my being able to see and to hear this morning. I'm blessed because You are a forgiving God and an understanding God. You have done so much for me and You keep on blessing me. Forgive me this day for everything I have done, said or thought that was not pleasing to you...I ask now for Your forgiveness.

Please keep me safe from all danger and harm. Help me to start this day with a new attitude and plenty of gratitude. Let me make the best of each and every day to clear my mind so that I can hear from You.

Please broaden my mind that I can accept all things.

Let me not whine and whimper over things I have no control over. Let me continue to see sin through God's eyes and acknowledge it as evil. And when I sin, let me repent, and confess with my mouth my wrongdoing, and receive the forgiveness of God.

And when this world closes in on me, let me remember Jesus' example -- to slip away and find a quiet place to pray. It's the best response when I'm pushed beyond my limits. I know that when I can't pray, You listen to my heart. Continue to use me to do Your will.

Continue to bless me that I may be a blessing to others. Keep me strong that I may help the weak. Keep me uplifted that I may have words of encouragement for others. I pray for those who are lost and can't find their way. I pray for those who are misjudged and misunderstood. I pray for those who don't know You intimately. I pray for those who don't believe. But I thank you that I believe.

I believe that God changes people and God changes things. I pray for all my sisters and brothers; for each and every family member in their household. I pray for peace, love and joy in their homes that they are out of debt and all their needs are met.

I pray that every ear that hears this knows there is no problem, circumstance, or situation greater than God. Every battle is in Your hands for You to fight. I pray that these words be received into the hearts of every eye that sees them and every mouth that confesses them willingly…in the name of the Father and of the Son and of the Holy Spirit Amen.

Prayer of Saint Teresa of Avila

Let nothing disturb you,
Let nothing frighten you,
All things are passing away:
God never changes.
Patience obtains all things.
Whoever has God lacks nothing;
God alone suffices.

The Miracle Prayer

Lord Jesus, I come before you just as I am. I am sorry for my sins and I repent of my sins, please forgive me. In your name, I forgive all others for what they have done against me. I renounce Satan, the evil spirits and all their works. Lord, I give you my entire self, now and forever. Jesus, I invite you into my life, I accept you as my Lord, God and Savior. Heal me, change me, and strengthen me in body, soul and spirit.

Come Lord Jesus, cover me with your precious blood and fill me with your Holy Spirit, I love you Lord Jesus. I Praise you Jesus. I thank you Jesus; I shall follow you all the days of my life — Amen.

Holy Mary, my Mother, queen of peace, Saint Michael, Saint Gabriel, Saint Raphael, all you holy angels and saints, pray for me — Amen.

Litany for the Church in Our Time

Lord, have mercy.
Christ, have mercy.

Lord, have mercy on us.
Christ, Divine Founder of the Church, hear us.

Christ, Who didst warn of false prophets, graciously hear us.

God, the Father of Heaven, have mercy on us.

God, the Son, Redeemer of the World, have mercy on us.

God, the Holy Ghost, have mercy on us.

Holy Trinity, One God, have mercy on us.

Holy Mary, Mother of God, pray for us.

St. Joseph, Patron of the Universal Church, pray for us.

St. Michael, Defender in Battle, pray for us.

St. Peter, the Rock upon which Christ built His Church, pray for us.

St. Paul, Protector of the Faithful Remnant, pray for us.

St. Francis of Assisi, re-builder of the Church, pray for us.

St. Anthony, Hammer of Heretics, pray for us.

St. Pius V, Restorer of the beauty of the Sacred Liturgy, pray for us.

St. Pius X, Foe of Modernism, pray for us.

All ye Holy Angels and Archangels, pray that we may resist the snares of the Devil.

St. Catherine of Siena, pray that Christ's Vicar may oppose the spirit of the world.

St. John Fisher, pray that bishops may have the courage to combat heresy and irreverence.

St. Francis Xavier, pray that zeal for souls may be rekindled in the clergy.

St. Charles Borromeo, pray that seminaries may be protected from false teachings.

St. Vincent de Paul, pray that seminarians may return to a life of prayer and meditation.

St. Therese of the Child Jesus, pray that religious may rediscover their vocation of love and sacrifice.

St. Thomas More, pray that the laity may not succumb to the Great Apostasy.

St. Francis de Sales, pray that the Catholic press may again become a vehicle of Truth.

St. John Bosco, pray that our children may be protected from immoral and heretical instruction.

St. Pascal, pray that profound reverence for the Most Blessed Sacrament may be restored.

St. Dominic, pray that we may ever treasure the Holy Rosary.

Lamb of God, Who taketh away the sins of the world, spare us, O Lord.

Lamb of God, Who taketh away the sins of the world, graciously hear us.

Lamb of God, Who taketh away the sins of the world, have mercy on us.

Christ, hear us. Christ, graciously hear us.

Pray for us, O Holy Mother of God, that we may be made worthy of the promises of Christ.

Let Us Pray.

Jesus, our God, in these dark hours when Thy Mystical Body is undergoing its own Crucifixion, and when it would almost seem to be abandoned by God the Father, have mercy, we beg of Thee, on Thy suffering Church. Send down upon us the Divine Consoler, to enlighten our minds and strengthen our wills.

Thou, O Second Person of the Most Holy Trinity, Who canst neither deceive nor be deceived, have promised to be with Thy Church until the end of time. Give us a mighty Faith that we may not falter; help us to do Thy Holy Will always, especially during these hours of grief and uncertainty. May Thy Most Sacred Heart and the Immaculate and Sorrowful Heart of Thy Holy Mother be our sure refuge in time and in eternity. —Amen.

Section 4

Catholic Faith Facts

There are Three Ways God Answers Prayer

1. No, because I love you too much and your request is not according to my will.
2. Yes, but not yet.
3. Yes, that request is in accord with my will.

Remember what we ask for in prayer, God might not grant that day, but he will always answer us in his own time and way.

Biblical Reasons Why God Does Not Answer Prayer

Deuteronomy 1:43-45 (NAB) I gave you this warning but you would not listen. You defied the LORD's command and arrogantly went off into the hill country. Then the Amorites living in that hill country came out against you and put you to flight the way bees do, cutting you down in Seir as far as Hormah. On your return you wept before the LORD, but the LORD did not listen to your voice or give ear to you. *The Lord will not listen to the arrogant and those that defy his commandments.*

Deuteronomy 18:9-12 (NAB) When you come into the land which the LORD, your God, is giving you, you shall not learn to imitate the abominations of the nations there. Let there not be found among you anyone who causes their son or daughter to pass through the fire, or practices divination, or is a soothsayer, augur, or sorcerer, or who casts spells, consults ghosts and spirits, or seeks oracles from the dead. Anyone who does such things is an abomination to the LORD, and because of such abominations the LORD, your God, is dispossessing them before you. *Anyone who practices the dark pagan occultic religions is an offense to God. Such person will not be heard by God because they are an abomination.*

2 Chronicles 7:14 (NAB) if then my people, upon whom my name has been pronounced, humble themselves and pray, and seek my face and turn from their evil ways, I will hear them from Heaven and pardon their sins and heal their land. *You must seek Gods face and turn away from your sin in order for God to hear your prayer.*

Job 27:8-9 (NAB) For what hope has the impious when he is cut off, when God requires his life? Will God then listen to his cry when distress comes upon him. *God does not hear the cry of those who are irreligious and lack reverence for the Almighty.*

Job 35:12-13 (NAB) Though thus they cry out, he does not answer because of the pride of the wicked. But it is idle to say God does not hear or that the Almighty does not take notice. God does not hear the plea of the proud.

Psalm 32:2-5 (NAB) Blessed is the man to whom the LORD imputes no guilt, in whose spirit is no deceit. Because I kept silent, my bones wasted away; I groaned all day long. For day and night your hand was heavy upon me; my strength withered as in dry summer heat. Then I declared my sin to you; my guilt I did not hide. I said, "I confess my transgression to the LORD," and you took away the guilt of my sin. *We must confess our sins to be forgiven.*

Psalm 66:17-18 (NAB) I cried aloud to him, and he was extolled with my tongue. If I had cherished iniquity in my heart, the Lord would not have listened. *If you have unconfessed unrepentant sin in your heart the Lord will not listen to you.*

Proverbs 1:28-33 (NAB) Then they will call me, but I will not answer; they will seek me, but will not find me, Because they hated knowledge, and the fear of the LORD they did not choose. They ignored my counsel, they spurned all my reproof; Well, then, they shall eat the fruit of their own way, and with their own devices be glutted. For the straying of the naive kills them, the smugness of fools destroys them. But whoever obeys me dwells in security, in peace, without fear of harm." *God will not hear those who disobey him, hate knowledge and have a superiority complex.*

Proverbs 15:29 (NAB) The LORD is far from the wicked, but he hears the prayer of the righteous. *The Lord will not hear the prayer of the wicked and unrighteous.*

Proverbs 21:13 (NAB) He who closes his ear to the cry of the poor will himself cry out and not be heard. V*ery clear, if you have contempt for the poor, the Lord will not hear your prayer.*

Isaiah 1:15-16 (RSV) When you spread forth your hands, I will hide my eyes from you; even though you make many prayers, I will not listen; your hands are full of blood. Wash yourselves; make yourselves clean; remove the evil of your doings from before my eyes; cease to do evil. *God will not hear the prayers of unrepentant murderers like terrorists, serial killers, and narcotic cartel mobsters.*

Malachi 2:13-16 (NAB) This also you do: the altar of the LORD you cover with tears, weeping, and groaning, Because the Lord no longer takes note of your offering or accepts it favorably from your hand. And you say, "Why?"– Because the LORD is witness between you and the wife of your youth with whom you have broken faith, though she is your companion, your covenanted wife. Did he not make them one, with flesh and spirit? And what does the One require? Godly offspring! You should be on guard, then, for your life, and do not break faith with the wife of your youth. For I hate divorce, says the LORD, the God of Israel...*The Lord will not* *hear the prayer of an adulterous man who leaves the wife that he is lawfully married to.*

Matthew 6:14-15 (NAB) If you forgive others their transgressions, your heavenly Father will forgive you. But if you do not forgive others, neither will your Father forgive your transgressions. *We must forgive others in order to enter Heaven where there is only pure love. Also, purely from a mental health standpoint, When you refuse to forgive someone, your allowing them to rent space in your mind, that's not good.*

Matthew 27:41-44 (NAB) Likewise the chief priests with the scribes and elders mocked him and said, "He saved others; he cannot save himself. So he is the king of Israel! Let him come down from the cross now, and we will believe in him. He trusted in God; let him deliver him now if he wants him. For he said, 'I am the Son of God.'" The revolutionaries who were crucified with him also kept abusing him in the same way. *Those who reject Jesus Christ will not be forgiven and will not be saved (cf. Matthew 10:32-33).*

Mark 11:25 (NAB) When you stand to pray, forgive anyone against whom you have a grievance, so that your heavenly Father may in turn forgive you your transgressions." *Nobody will get to Heaven that has bitterness and unforgiveness for someone in there heart.*

Luke 9:39-41 (NAB) For a spirit seizes him and he suddenly screams and it convulses him until he foams at the mouth; it releases him only with difficulty, wearing him out. I begged your disciples to cast it out but they could not." Jesus said in reply, "O faithless and perverse generation, how long will I be with you and endure you? Bring your son here." *The Lord will not listen to the prayers of faithless people.*

Luke 18:2-8 (NAB) "There was a judge in a certain town who neither feared God nor respected any human being. And a widow in that town used to come to him and say, 'Render a just decision for me against my adversary.' For a long time the judge was unwilling, but eventually he thought, 'While it is true that I neither fear God nor respect any human being, because this widow keeps bothering me I shall deliver a just decision for her lest she finally come and strike me.'" The Lord said, "Pay attention to what the dishonest judge says. Will not God then secure the rights of his chosen ones who call out to him day and night? Will he be slow to answer them? I tell you, he will see to it that justice is done for them speedily..." *God will answer those who pray to him without ceasing (cf. 1 Thessalonians 5:17).*

Acts 28:27 (NAB) Gross is the heart of this people; they will not hear with their ears; they have closed their eyes, so they may not see with their eyes and hear with their ears and understand with their heart and be converted, and I heal them. *God will not listen to unrepentant hard hearted people.*

2 Corinthians 12:7-10 (NAB) And to keep me from being too elated by the abundance of revelations, a thorn was given me in the flesh, a messenger of Satan, to harass me, to keep me from being too elated. Three times I besought the Lord about this, that it should leave me; but he said to me, "My grace is sufficient for you, for my power is made perfect in weakness." I will all the more gladly boast of my weaknesses, that the power of Christ may rest upon me. For the sake of Christ, then, I am content with weaknesses, insults, hardships, persecutions, and calamities; for when I am weak, then I am strong. *Sometimes God will not hear your prayer because he wants you to draw closer to him and detach yourself more and more from this world. He will give you the grace to carry your cross.*

Ephesians 5:10 (NAB) Try to learn what is pleasing to the Lord. *God will listen to prayer that is pleasing to him.*

James 1:5-8 (NAB) But if any of you lacks wisdom, he should ask God who gives to all generously and ungrudgingly, and he will be given it. But he should ask in faith, not doubting, for the one who doubts is like a wave of the sea that is driven and tossed about by the wind. For that person must not suppose that he will receive anything from the Lord, since he is a man of two minds, unstable in all his ways. *God will not hear the prayers of a lukewarm Christian who lives his life sitting on a fence. (cf. Revelation 3:15-16)*

James 4:2-4 (NAB) You covet but do not possess. You kill and envy but you cannot obtain; you fight and wage war. You do not possess because you do not ask. You ask but do not receive, because you ask wrongly, to spend it on your passions. Adulterers! Do you not know that to be a lover of the world means enmity with God? Therefore, whoever wants to be a lover of the world makes himself an enemy of God. *God will not listen to people who ask for things simply to titilate their disordered passions.*

1 Peter 3:7 (NAB) Likewise, you husbands should live with your wives in understanding, showing honor to the weaker female sex, since we are joint heirs of the gift of life, so that your prayers may not be hindered. *If a husband treats his wife disrespectfully like a 2nd class citizen their prayers will not be answered.*

1 Peter 3:10-12 (NAB) "Whoever would love life and see good days must keep the tongue from evil and the lips from speaking deceit, must turn from evil and do good, seek peace and follow after it. For the eyes of the Lord are on the righteous and his ears turned to their prayer, but the face of the Lord is against evildoers." *The Lord will not listen to the prayers of wicked evildoers.*

1 John 5:14 (NAB) And we have this confidence in him, that if we ask anything according to his will, he hears us. *God will not hear our prayer if it is not according to his will. God's will for us is that we become 'holy' (cf. 1 Thessalonians 4:3).*

Without Prayer Man Becomes a Beast

What does God do after the sixth day?

.... And He rested on the seventh day from all His work which He had done. So God blessed the seventh day and hallowed it, making it holy, because on it God rested from all His work which He had done in creation.

—Genesis 2:1

Now, why did God rest? Was He worn out? Was He a tired God? [No] Why would God bless and sanctify the seventh day, the Sabbath? He is showing Himself to be a Father. Giving to us an example of behavior he wants from us who are in His image and likeness.

"Man is not made for the Sabbath," Jesus says, "but the Sabbath is made for man." To tell us that we are more than Beasts. We were created with the beasts on the sixth day, but we are created for the Father on the seventh. The Sabbath is a day of worship whereby we lay hold of our status as divine children.

What becomes of man when he refuses to worship, when he refuses God as Father and His covenant? He reverts and becomes like a beast in a sixth day kind of life, not the seventh day kind of life.

Gentiles are described, people who are out of covenant with God, who don't worship God, people who worship themselves and their own works, like Goliath. How tall is Goliath? Six cubits. The 'six' stands out.

When Nebuchadnezzar tyrannically abused, dominated, and enslaved the Jews, he made a huge statue of himself which Daniel notes was 60 by 6 cubits, because he was a beast, and in Daniel 7, Nebuchadnezzar is described like a beast, because he is reverting by refusing God as Father.

And Revelation 13, the number of the beast is what? 666. Why? Because the anti-Christ wants to turn us away from being God's children. Turn us away from worship. And so we get the number – because to buy or sell, you need 'the number.' In other words, people who worship work are animalistic. They are not "productive." They are beast-like.

What we were made for is being in God's family, which is a gift, that we only receive when we put our work down and receive God's work, God's grace. We deceive ourselves when we think that we can work our way into heaven, or that we can earn God's grace. The grace of sonship is pure gift. Children do not work their way into family; they are born into family. [We are born into God's family through Baptism, of water and the Holy Spirit.]

Why does God create in six days and then rest on the seventh? God shows us how He created in order to show men and women how they can re-create. This applies to our work, our recreation, our rest, our worship.

[All of the above taken from Dr Scott Hahn's *Genesis Bible Study* The Covenant as a Family Affair; A University Level Course in Scripture. Group Study Guide from St. Joseph's Communications 2010.]

CCC #2096 – Adoration is the first act of the virtue of religion. To adore God is to acknowledge him as God, as the Creator and Savior, the Lord and Master of everything that exists, as infinite and merciful Love. "You shall worship the Lord your God, and him only shall you serve," says Jesus, citing Deuteronomy.

The Dark Night of the Senses & Dark Night of the Soul

The following is taken from Dr. Taylor Marshall's on-line article entitled, "The Difference Between Dark Night of the Soul and Dark Night of the Senses (according to St. John of the Cross":[45]

> According to Saint Paul and Saint John of the Cross and the masters of Mystical Theology, such as John Tauler, the spiritual life consists in three ages:
>
> - Beginners (Purgative Way)
> - Proficients (Illuminative Way)
> - Perfect (Unitive Way)
>
> Incidentally, by Perfect we mean not absolute perfection (like the saints in Heaven) but relative perfection.
>
> These three ages mirror natural human life:
>
> - Childhood
> - Adolescence
> - Adulthood
>
> Just as these three stages are transitioned by a crisis, so also progress in the spiritual life is marked by crisis.
>
> Saint John of the Cross, the Doctor of the Church with regard to Mystical Theology, teaches that the transition from the Purgative to the Illuminative is occasioned by the "Dark Night of the Senses" and the transition from the Illuminative to the Unitive is

occasioned by the "Dark Night of the Soul."

- Beginners (Purgative Way)
- **Dark Night of Senses**
- Proficients (Illuminative Way)

- **Dark Night of the Soul**
- Perfect (Unitive Way)

The Dark Night of the Senses is the crisis in which God purposefully withdraws consolations of the senses. Warm fuzzies in prayer. Discursive pictorial visions in the imagination, physical comfort, lack of external distraction.

This is very difficult because the Christian begins to worry that he is regressing or has done something to lose God's favor. Instead, God is preparing him to enter more deeply in the love of God. The soul learns to seek the God of consolation, but not merely the consolations of God. Perhaps this Dark Night of the Senses is one of the most misunderstood elements of daily Christian living.

The Dark Night of the Spirit or Dark Night of the Soul is a crushing desolation where the soul learns to love the cross of Christ. With a desire to be more like Christ and to share in His life, the perfect learn to love persecution, humiliations, disgrace, and other problems in life since they see in them a perfect conformity to God. Two well-known modern examples are Saint Pio and Saint Therese.

We see this state of perfection in the Apostles:

> "And calling in the apostles, after they had scourged them, they charged them that they should not speak at all in the name of Jesus.

> And they dismissed them. And they indeed went from the presence of the council, rejoicing that they were accounted worthy to suffer reproach for the name of Jesus."
>
> —Acts 5:40–41, D-R

Saints Peter and John rejoiced in their sufferings. This is not something naturally, but something utterly supernatural – it is a sign of the unitive way. The Apostles, we might say, went through the Dark Night of the Senses from Good Friday till Easter and the Dark Night of the Soul from the Ascension to Pentecost. This, at least, is the position of Fr Garrigou-Lagrange.

The following is taken from: Dr Mark Miravelle's online course "Christian Spirituality"[46]. Dr. Miravele writes:

> Fr. Garrigous Lagrange (Dominican theologian); one of the foremost experts in this century on dogmatic theology and the mystical life. He had a pupil we know as Pope John Paul II. The Pope when he was a priest studying for his doctorate was sent to the Angelicum under this great theologian Fr Garrigou Lagrange, and he received his doctorate from him. Fr Garrigou Lagrange wrote many books, one just came back into print by TAN publishers which is called, *The 3 Ages of the Interior Life*. He writes that conversion is an ongoing process. We must experience the power of God more than just once, the Lord must invade our world. This phenomenon must be experienced as an adult. The 3 stages of the interior life are: (1) The purgative stage – where we recognize that we are sinners and we are purged from the love of sin. (2) The illuminative stage – where we are enlightened or illumined about the truth of God in Christ. We're falling in love with God

(3) The unitive stage – where our will is so united to Gods will that you want what God wants no matter what suffering this may entail. Very few people ever reach this stage of maturity where they can truly say the words of St Paul in Philippians 1:21 "For me to live is Christ and to die is gain…" or John 3:30 "he must increase and I must decrease…" or Galatians 2:20 "it is no longer I who live but Christ who lives in me…" God is pouring himself into us.

The dark night of the sense is the transition between the 1st and 2nd stage, dark night of the sense God is pulling back from us, no more candy, the dark night of the soul feels like God totally abandons us. It's a time of growing up and trust by faith. These stages from the 1, 2, 3 are not clear cut, they are kind of organic. We take 2 steps forward and 1 step backwards.

In the beginning stage of our spiritual life we really feel the presence of God. As we start maturing God starts pulling away from us. God wants us to be rooted in God versus sentiments. God is teaching us to grow up. The dark night of the soul is the transition between the 2nd and 3rd stage. God is there no matter how we feel.

What are the Dangers that can Arise During the Dark Night of the Soul?

This is the bridge to the unitive way. This is a series of passive purgation's that seeks to complete what was started in the 1st dark night. The 1st night sought perfection of sense (lower part of the soul), the 2nd purification seeks the internal faculties of the soul (the highest abilities: the intellect and the will). The defects in this stage are: 1) involuntary distractions in prayer, 2) a dullness in prayer – a full sensitivity of taking for granted spiritual things, 3) a temptation to over zealousness instead of fraternal charity, 4) Lastly, a final purification of the will from an unconscious egoism.

God must take complete possession of the soul and occupy it. These souls can get puffed up with pride in an undetected manner, ergo, the need for the final process of purification. This stage is a purification of the interior faculties: will, intellect and memory (the powers of the soul).

Why is the dark night of the soul the bridge between the purgative way and the illuminative way?

The following is taken from the "Understanding the Dark Night of the Soul"[47] by Emily Stimpson, OSV contributing editor:

> The purgative way last until a certain bridge in the spiritual life – this bridge is called the dark night of the soul. The 1st dark night of the soul is where the Holy Spirit begins to purify the soul from sense desires alien to the Christian life. The dark night of the soul is the beginning of the mystical life; it is therefore technically the beginning of the illuminative way. Once the dark night begins the person is no longer in control – they do not begin the purgation and they have no power of ending it unless they decide to regress and return to an earlier less mature state of their walk with the Lord. To recap – the dark night (of sense) is the bridge between the purgative and the illuminative way. The 2nd dark night (of soul) is the bridge between the illuminative and unitive. This is the dark night of the soul, the purification between the intellect and the will.

"Understanding the 'dark night of the soul' The feeling of spiritual emptiness, or being abandoned by God, is natural in the process of growing closer to Christ."

It is Necessary

Every fallen human being has disordered desires and attachments. We love what we shouldn't love, or we love what we should but in the wrong way. We seek our own comfort, our own pleasure, our own will. We value what we want more than we value what God wants. We do wrong, even if only in our hearts.

But we can't do wrong and stand before God. We can't even want to do wrong and stand before God. A prerequisite for seeing God face to face is that every attachment to sin, both in our lives and in our hearts, must be broken. If we want to become saints, we have to desire only God's will. And we have to desire God's will not out of fear of hell, but rather out of love for heaven, out of love for God. Some of that breaking we do, as we learn to avoid vice and pursue virtue. But some of that breaking only God can do. The dark night of the soul is, in part, how he does that. By seemingly withdrawing all spiritual consolations — all the little comforts and supports that typically come from pursuing a relationship with him — and allowing an almost crushing sense of abandonment to descend upon us, he purifies our desires and prepares us for heaven.

It is Unique

The dark night of the soul looks different in different lives. Laypersons don't necessarily experience the dark night the way religious do. Nor do active religious necessarily experience the dark night the way contemplatives do. Some people experience it primarily through external circumstances. They find themselves persecuted or afflicted. In the midst of those afflictions, all calls for help go unanswered. To the person passing through this type of dark night, it feels like God has left them to deal with their cross on their own.

Others experience the dark night through temptations: Temptations to pride, vanity, anger, sexual sin, and even unbelief assail them. Then, there are those who experience the dark night of the soul mainly through inner desolation: The gates of heaven seem barred against them, and no matter how much they pray, no consolation seemingly comes. Lastly, there are those who experience the dark night as a combination of all three: trials, temptations and abandonment.

Likewise, for some, the dark night comes but once. For others, it comes many times. Usually, it lasts for only a short while. Occasionally, it lasts much longer. But when it finally ends, it ends for good. A definitive work has been accomplished in the soul.

It is Unpredictable

The dark night of the soul doesn't come at the beginning of one's journey to God. Traditionally, spiritual directors identify three primary stages (or ways) of growth in holiness. The first is the purgative way, where we break habits of vice, acquire habits of virtue and learn to live a Catholic life. The second is the illuminative way, where we grow in virtue, charity and the life of prayer. And the third is the unitive way, where our wills and hearts move in perfect harmony with God's.

Near the end of the purgative stage, we experience

a type of dark night — a time of trial and affliction where it feels as if God no longer loves us. This dark night, however, is not the dark night of the soul. Rather, it's the dark night of the senses.

In the dark night of the senses, God purifies us of our attachments to the things of the world — physical comfort, physical pleasure, material success, popular acclaim — as well as of our consolations in prayer. Sorrows afflict us, and things that used to comfort us — food, sex, shopping, compliments, even the liturgy — no longer do. Through this dark night, God prepares us for the illuminative way and a deeper, more contemplative life of prayer.

The dark night of the soul occurs at the end of the illuminative way, as we prepare to enter the unitive way. During this dark night, God roots out our deepest attachments to sin and self, and the desolation that accompanies that rooting out is overwhelming and crushing. More than just a lack of consolation, this dark night plunges a soul into an abyss of darkness and nothingness, essentially revealing to us what we are without God and preparing us to not only carry our crosses, but to love our crosses and carry them joyfully in union with Christ.

It isn't Depression

From the outside, depression and the dark night of the soul bear a striking resemblance to one another. And they're not entirely separate things. As St. John of the Cross noted long ago, depression (or as they called it in the 17th century, melancholia) can go hand in hand with a dark night, whether by exacerbating it or resulting from it.

But while clinical depression is triggered by an objectively sad event (losing a loved one, fatal illness, etc.) or by a biochemical problem, the dark night of the soul is purely an act of God; it is God working in our souls to draw us closer to him. Likewise, while depression weighs down both body and soul, eventually rendering those who suffer from it unable to go about the normal business of their life, throughout the dark night, the spirit stays strong, and those suffering through it can perform great works of charity and service. They remain active and don't experience the same temptations to total self-loathing or suicide that those struggling with depression suffer, nor do they lose their faith in the midst of the dark night. Belief remains.

It isn't evil

The dark night of the soul is not an evil to be endured; it's a good for which we should be grateful. Of course, it doesn't always seem that way. The thought of plunging into a spiritual abyss and losing all the sweetness in our relationship with God strikes few as appealing. But neither does surgery. Having cancer removed from our bodies isn't a fun process. Nevertheless, we submit to the surgeon's knife readily and quickly, knowing that the sooner we have the surgery, the sooner we can live a healthy, full life.

What's true on the natural level is true on the supernatural level. If we want to become the people God made us to be and live the lives he made us to live, we must let him excise sin and unhealthy attachments from our souls. There's no getting around it. Before we can enter heaven, it has to happen. It can happen in this life or it can happen in the next — in purgatory. But here is better. For the sooner we let God root out unhealthy attachments, the sooner we can get on with the business of being saints. And there's no better business than that.

The Results of Eucharistic Adoration

1. Each hour you spend with JESUS in the Blessed Sacrament He will give you a deep Peace within your heart. "Come to Me all of you who are weary and find life burdensome and I will give you rest" (Matthew 11:28).

2. JESUS will give you all the graces (strength) you need to live an obedient and faithful life. "My grace is sufficient for you, for my power is made perfect in (your) weakness" (2 Corinthians 12:9).

3. For Peace in our Country! "If my people…humble themselves and pray and seek my face, and turn from their wicked ways, then I will hear them from heaven, and will forgive their sin and heal their land" (2 Chronicles 7:14).

4. Each hour you spend with JESUS on earth will leave your soul everlastingly MORE BEAUTIFUL and GLORIOUS. "They who humble themselves shall be exulted" (Luke 18:14). "All of us gazing on the Lord's glory with unveiled faces, are being transformed from glory to glory into His very image" (2 Corinthians 3:18).

5. JESUS will Bless you and your Family for this Holy hour you spend with Him in the Blessed Sacrament. "Blessed are they who do not see and yet believe…" (John 20:29). "What is needed is trust…" (Mark 5:36). "Behold I come to make all things new" (Revelation 21:5).

6. Each moment you spend with JESUS in the Blessed Sacrament brings joy, pleasure and delight to His Sacred Heart. "My joy, my delight, my pleasure is to be with you" (Proverbs 8:31).

7. Just as you can't be exposed to the sun without receiving its rays, neither can you be exposed to JESUS in the Blessed Sacrament without receiving the divine rays of His grace, His love and His peace. "Christ is truly Emmanuel, that is 'God with us' day and night, He is in our midst. He dwells with us full of grace" (Pope Paul VI – *Mysterium Fidei*).

Points to Remember

1. This hour in Eucharistic Adoration JESUS wants you to spend it with Him anyway you want.

2. You may bring your own prayer books, use the books in the Chapel, read the Bible, pray the rosary.

3. Or just sit, relax, be quiet and be still and enjoy the sweet peace that comes from simply being in the presence of God Almighty.

4. You may feel that you cant pray, don't be discouraged. The fact that you took time out to spend with JESUS in the Blessed Sacrament pleases the LORD very much, and is in itself a prayer of great faith.

I gave you some spiritual direction on how to overcome stress and anxiety, however, on a natural level you should also try to:

1. Laugh – laughing actually lowers your cortisol levels while boosting your endorphins, which helps improve your mood.

2. Focus on your Health, moderate walking or swimming are fantastic for clearing your mind of worries. People show health and mood improvements with as little as a 10 minute walk each day.

3. Add Stress Busting Foods to Your Diet. Fruits and vegetables, especially asparagus, avocado, blueberries, oranges, and spinach, are full of nutrients and antioxidants that improve mood and general heart health. Almonds, salmon, oatmeal are also excellent foods to include in your stress busting diet.

4. Get rid of unhealthy thought habits. Become aware of your internal dialogue, and if you find yourself engaging in negative thinking, calmly direct your thoughts to something positive. For example, if you find yourself reliving a negative experience and discounting your successes at the end of the day, put a positive spin on it. Count your successes and let the negative go, especially if you cannot change it. Stress is a necessary part of our life. It keeps us alert, safe and sometimes excited. Each of us has our own limits of how much stress we can handle."

   [List taken from Holman, Dr Ron. "Coping Skils to Deal With Daily Stress." *The ALADS Dispatcher* 1 Aug. 2014, Summer 2014 ed., Managed Behavorial Health Care Services sec.: 16-17. Print.]

The Benefits of Attending Church

1. Church attendance is the number one predictor of marital stability and happiness.[48]

2. Attending church is helpful in the prevention of cancer, heart disease and mental illness.[49]

3. Teens who attend church are four times less likely to commit suicide.[50]

4. Patients who suffer from depression heal much more rapidly if they practice their religious faith. Religious people who are depressed have a shorter time for recovery.[51]

5. Religious people spend less time in the hospital, are healthier, recover faster, and generally handle life's ups and downs in more positive ways. Other studies report that religious people tend to live 30 percent longer and experience better physical and mental health. They also have better marriages, better families and use less addictive substances.[52]

6. There is lower blood pressure among men who attend church verse those who do not.[53]

7. Traditional married family has the highest family yearly income. The intact married family has a higher income than the - the average stepfamily, the cohabitating family and the separated or divorced single-parent family.[54]

8. Church-goers have fewer heart attacks than non-church goers.[55]

9. Young men who were raised in intact families and worshipped weekly have a higher income as adults than young men who came from broken families and never worshiped.[56]

10. Cities with high church attendance have the lowest crime rates.[57]

11. People attending church are physically healthier and less depressed than their non believing neighbors.[58]

12. In a study of the religious life of alcoholics, results showed that the majority who abuse alcohol do not have a religious commitment; 89% of alcoholics surveyed in the study stated they lost interest in religion during their teenage years.[59]

13. University of California at Los Angeles School of Medicine found that alcohol abuse is 300 percent higher among those who do not attend church.[60]

14. Church attendance moves underprivileged out of poverty and into the middle class. Regular church attendance, for example, is particularly instrumental in helping young people to escape the poverty of inner-city life.[61]

15. There is an additional average life expectancy of eight years for people of faith and prayer that go to Church.[62]

16. Religious involvement significantly decreases sexual promiscuity.[63]

17. Those attending church are more likely to remain married and have a better sex-life which indicates that religion is an important part of marital happiness.[64]

18. Married couples report greater sexual satisfaction. The highest levels of sexual satisfaction were reported by individuals who were in married, monogamous relationships, while those who were single or cohabitating reported slightly lower levels of sexual satisfaction.[65]

19. People who are addicted to any destructive or immoral behavior have an advantage when they go to Church based programs.[66]

20. Highly religious moral families enjoy more success and happiness and are less likely to divorce and engage in narcotic substance abuse.[67]

21. Studies show that prayer helps people heal, even when they don't know they are being prayed for. Studies also found something else, the ninety adults who prayed for the subject group also improved in health![68]

22. Religious elderly have shorter hospital stays and lower health care costs as compared to non-religious elderly.[69]

23. Marriage is associated with a lower mortality risk. Compared to married individuals, those who have never been married had nearly twice the mortality risk. Divorced or separated individuals ran a mortality risk more than 50 percent higher than those who were married.[70]

24. Those attending church are less likely to require antibiotics after an illness.[71]

25. Fathers that go to church spend more time with children.[72]

The Power of Leadership

Never underestimate the power of your leadership as a man. Here's a telling statistic about the influence of a father.

> If a father does not go to Church, no matter how faithful his wife's devotions, only one child in fifty (2%) will become a regular Church goer. If a father does go regularly, regardless of the practice of the mother, between 66 to 75% of their children will become regular churchgoers.[73]

What Prayer Does to Your Brain

Nick Tate publisher of the Newsmax's *The Mind Health Report* wrote:

> The mainstream media routinely avoid this subject, even though statistics show three out of every four Americans pray on a daily or weekly basis. Let me be clear. We're not promoting any specific religion or spiritual practice. But rather, we wanted to see what neuroscientists learned from their laboratory tests and controlled double-blind medical studies regarding these questions…
>
> Frankly, were surprised and excited by what we found. Because not only can you measure prayer as brain activity, but prayer also has been scientifically proven to help:

- Reduce stress and lower your blood pressure…
- Boost your resistance to illness and disease…
- Neutralize harmful negative emotions…
- Enhance your memory and mental function…
- Prevent dementia and Alzheimer's disease…
- Decrease your suffering from pain…
- Give you a healthier, longer, and happier life…

> Let's begin by defining "prayer."
>
> At *The Mind Health Report*, our goal is to help you

achieve better physical, mental, and emotional health through good brain health. So, for the purposes of our research, we defined "praying" as any mental activity that includes:

1. **Traditional prayers** practiced by people of religious faith, such as making a petition to God, or expressing gratitude for God's goodness.

2. **Meditation**, or contemplative reflection on a power greater than oneself, which can be God, the Universe, or all Life.

3. **Focused positive thinking**, such as speaking affirmations, setting worthwhile goals, and maintaining positive thoughts and speech.

4. **Attending a church or synagogue service** and praying and singing with the congregation.

Of course, if you're a person who prays regularly, you already know that prayer has brought many positive benefits to your life. Yet what you probably don't know — but will discover today — **is the Brain Science Behind Prayer.**

Let's begin with an illustration of the brain.

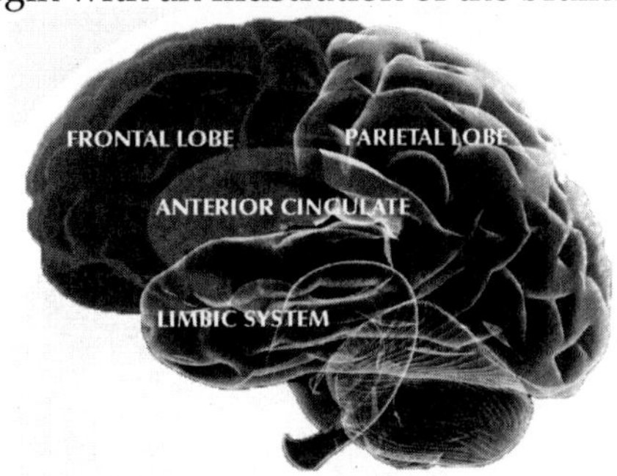

Prayer and spiritual practices impact the different parts of your brain, and that, in turn, affects your physical and mental health.

Note the four major areas of the brain: the frontal lobe, the anterior cingulate, the parietal lobe, and the limbic system, which is comprised of several smaller parts.

Each of these areas plays an important role, but according to Dr. Newberg, two of the four parts are much more important to your health and happiness, especially as you age. And the good news is this, Prayer Stimulates the Parts of Your Brain That Help Keep You Healthy and Happy!

First, your frontal lobe, which is located just behind your forehead, is activated when you focus your attention, or when you plan, reason, read, or speak.

Obviously, this area is extremely important, as these are things you do almost every waking hour of every day.

But the danger is that the frontal lobe can shrink with age, and this shrinkage is associated with memory loss, mental decline, and even dementia and Alzheimer's.

Wouldn't it be wonderful to avoid this life-robbing mental decline? Well, now you can. You see, *prayer stimulates your frontal lobe, helps keep it healthy, and prevents age-related shrinkage.*

This is one of Dr. Andrew Newberg's most exciting findings, and he was able to repeat the result, again and again, as he monitored brain waves in the frontal lobe of his subjects as they prayed. However,

Dr. Newberg discovered that casual praying for just a few minutes per day had no significant impact on the frontal lobe. To get good results, he observed that his subjects needed to pray for a specific minimum number of minutes per day — or longer.

How long? In the report — '**Strengthen Your Brain Through the Power of Prayer**' — you'll discover exactly how many minutes per day you'll need to pray to gain this valuable anti-aging benefit. I'll give you a hint…It's more than 5 minutes, but not nearly as long as you'd spend vacuuming the house or washing the car. (My guess would be from 15 to 20 minutes, the time it takes to pray the rosary).

Next, let's move on to the anterior cingulate, the area of the brain that's activated when we feel empathy and compassion for others.

This part of our brain is what distinguishes us from animals. Dr. Newberg calls it our "neurological heart."

And the good news is that prayer activates your anterior cingulate, which helps you to feel compassion for others and a loving connection to God, or all Life. This, as you'll see in a moment, has many positive health benefits.

But let's continue now and consider two parts of your brain that are sometimes useful, but when unnecessarily activated can actually cause bodily and mental harm. Plus, why you're better off with less activity in these areas of your brain…

First are your parietal lobes, which give you a sense of yourself separate from other people and things in the world.

This area is important for spatial reckoning, physical self-awareness, and ego, but activity here can also give you a feeling of isolation and loneliness. And what's more, brain activity here is not associated with health benefits.

Fortunately, Dr. Newberg says *the time you spend praying, attending religious services, and even singing with the congregation deactivates your parietal lobes!*

This helps you to forget yourself and your problems, and instead to feel love and compassion for others, as well as a closeness to God, or all Life. Studies Show That Prayer Can Significantly Reduce How You Experience Pain. That's because prayer reduces activity in the parietal lobes, which causes you to have less awareness of yourself and more awareness of others.

After all, nothing is more important than brain health, because your brain affects every part of your body, as well as your feelings, even from one hour to the next. And when you understand how it works, you can control it in ways that dramatically improve your life.

Let's see more…

Finally, we must consider the limbic system, which frankly can be a real troublemaker.

You see, the limbic system includes several parts situated just above your spinal cord. This is the primitive area of your brain, sometimes called reptilian, because even reptiles have a limbic system.

The limbic system is where negative emotions are produced, such as anger, fear, and resentment, as well as anxiety, depression, and pessimism. Some of these emotions were necessary for the "fight or flight" response our ancestors needed to survive. But they have far less value in our modern civilized society, especially when you're mature and living a stable life.

Under such circumstances, negative emotions will unnecessarily cause physical and emotional harm.

How can you reduce these harmful negative emotions? According to Dr. Newberg, that's easy. *Prayer Turns Off Your Limbic System*. In fact, Dr. Newberg says that the more you diminish the activity in your parietal lobes and limbic system, at the same time you increase the activity in your frontal lobe and anterior cingulate — and as a result, you'll be HAPPIER AND HEALTHIER!

Simply put, prayer and spiritual practices increase activity in the areas of your brain that are most helpful to you, and diminish activity in the areas that are less helpful and even harmful.

Here are just a few of the amazing benefits of daily prayer...

- Increases your ability to feel love and compassion...
- Improves your memory and mental function...
- Prevents your frontal lobe from shrinking, which is the cause of memory loss, mental decline, and even Alzheimer's.
- Reduces stress and negative emotions, so you can feel at peace with yourself and others.

You can almost say that prayer is a kind of "fountain

of youth."

The following benefits have been reported in leading medical journals…

Two studies showed that praying for a person increases your capacity for forgiveness. And a third showed that forgiveness was associated with better overall health and satisfaction with life. (*Florida State University; Psychological Science*)

An analysis of 42 studies involving 125,000 people found that people who participate in spiritual practices are healthier and live longer. (*Health Psychology*)

Several studies have shown that prayer and other spiritual practices reduce or alleviate depression. (*The American Journal of Psychiatry*)

A study at Utah State University showed that older people with strong religious beliefs handled stress as well as persons 30 to 40 years younger and did not experience an elevation of blood pressure. (*Annals of Behavioral Medicine*)

Can You Imagine Getting Benefits Like These — All Through Daily Prayer?

Let's look at a few more…

In a study of 202 people suffering from chronic pain, researchers found that those who prayed or concentrated on positive thoughts were less affected by the pain and had a more positive outlook on life. (*Journal of Behavioral Medicine*)

In a study of 6,000 Californians between the ages of 21 and 75, those who attended weekly religious services reduced the risk of disease and death to the same extent as "not smoking or abusing alcohol." (*International Journal of Psychiatry in Medicine*)

Researchers at Duke University tracked nearly 4,000 people age 65 and older and found 40% less risk of elevated blood pressure among those who prayed daily and attended religious services weekly. (*International Journal of Psychiatry in Medicine*)

Researchers at Yale University School of Medicine studied more than 2,000 people over age 65 and found that those who attended religious services were less likely to lose their mental faculties or become physically disabled. (*Journal of Gerontology*)

Researchers at the University of Iowa found that people who make spiritual practices a regular part of their lives boost their resistance to viruses and other infections, which they concluded accounted for their healthier, longer lives. (*Health Psychology*)

And by contrast...

Researchers at the Harvard School of Public Health tracked 28,000 men between the ages of 42 and 77 for 10 years. They found those who had no close friends or spiritual practice in their lives had significantly increased risk of death from heart disease. (*American Journal of Epidemiology*)

[Article Taken from: Nick Tate; Newsmax Health - https://w3.mindhealthreport.com/Health/MHR/LP/MHR-Prayer-Video?dkt_nbr=8l2bahyy]

Bible Promises Give You an Attitude of Gratitude

1. Why should I say I can't when the bible says "I can do all things through him (Christ) who strengthens me" (Philippians 4:13).

2. Why should I despair when the bible says, "My God shall supply all my needs according to his riches in glory in Christ Jesus" (Philippians 4:19).

3. Why should I fear when the bible says, "God has not given me a spirit of fear, but of power, and of love and a sound mind" (2 Timothy 1:7).

4. Why should I doubt or lack faith knowing that "God has allotted to each a measure of faith" (Romans 12:3).

5. Why should I be weak when the bible says, "the Lord is the strength of my life (Psalm 27:1) and "the people who know their God will display strength and take action (Daniel 11:32).

6. Why should I allow Satan to have supremacy over my life, for "greater is he that is within me than he that is in the world" (1 John 4:4).

7. Why should I accept defeat when the bible says "thanks be to God who always leads us in his triumph in Christ, and manifests through the sweet aroma of the knowledge of him in every place (2 Corinthians 2:14).

8. Why should I lack wisdom when "Christ became to us wisdom from God (1 Corinthians 1:30) and "God

gives wisdom to all men generously and without reproach who ask him for it" (James 1:5).

9. Why should I accept sickness that is not of God when Jesus "took our infirmities and carried away our diseases" (Matthew 8:17) for "with his stripes I am healed" (Isaiah 53:5).

10. Why should I worry and fret when I can "cast all my anxiety upon Christ, because he cares for me" (1 Peter 5:7).

11. Why should I ever be in bondage, for "where the Spirit of the Lord is, there is liberty (2 Corinthians 3:7) and "it was for freedom that Christ set me free" (Galatians 5:1).

12. Why should I feel condemned when the bible says "there is no condemnation for those who are in Christ Jesus" (Romans 8:1).

13. Why should I ever feel alone when Jesus said "I am with you always, even to the end of the ages" (Matthew 28:20) and "I will never leave you nor forsake you" (Hebrew 13:5).

14. Why should I feel accursed or the victim of bad luck when the bible says that "Christ redeemed us from the curse of the law, being made a curse for us in order that in Christ Jesus we might receive the promise of the Spirit through faith" (Galatians 3:13,14).

15. Why should I feel worthless when the bible says, "For our sake he made him to be sin who knew no sin, so that in him we might become the righteousness of God" (2 Corinthians 5:21).

16. Why should I be sad, when like St Paul, "I have

learned, in whatever state I am to be content (Philippians 4:11).

17. Why should I ever have a persecution complex, "If God is for me, who can be against me" (Romans 8:31).

18. Why should I be confused, "God is not the author of confusion, but of peace" (1 Corinthians 14:33); and "now we have received not the spirit of the world, but the Spirit who is from God, that we might know the things freely given to us by God" (1 Corinthians 2:12).

19. Why should I feel like a failure when the bible says "In all these things we overwhelmingly conquer through him who loved us" (Romans 8:37).

20. Why should I let the pressures of life bother me when Jesus said, "In the world you have tribulation, but take courage, I have overcome the world" (John 16:33).

"The longer I live, the more I realize the impact of attitude on life. Attitude, to me, is more important than facts. It is more important than the past, the education, the money, than circumstances, than failure, than successes, than what other people think or say or do. It is more important than appearance, giftedness or skill. It will make or break a company... a church... a home. The remarkable thing is we have a choice everyday regarding the attitude we will embrace for that day. We cannot change our past... we cannot change the fact that people will act in a certain way. We cannot change the inevitable. The only thing we can do is play on the one string we have, and that is our attitude. I am convinced that life is 10% what happens to me and 90% of how I react to it. And so it is with you... we are in charge of our Attitudes."

—Chuck Swindoll

Attitude is Everything

It governs the way you perceive the world and the way the world perceives you. If we are to move forward into a new day with happiness and confidence, we need to adjust our attitudes to reflect feelings of positivity and abundance. Here are some tips for doing just that.

1. **Positive Internal Dialogue:** By speaking to yourself, you override your past negative programming by erasing or replacing it with a conscious, positive internal voice that helps you face new directions. Your internal conversation, that little voice you listen to all day long - acts like a seed in that it programs your brain and affects your behavior. Take a closer look at what you are saying to yourself.

2. **Enthusiasm** (greek "en theos" means "in God"): is a Vital tool for staying motivated. Enthusiasm is to attitude what breathing is to life. Enthusiasm enables you to apply your gifts more effectively. It's the burning desire that communicates commitment, determination and spirit. Enthusiasm means putting yourself in motion. It's an internal spirit that speaks through your actions from your commitment and your belief in what you are doing. It is one of the most empowering and attractive characteristics you can have.

   "Nothing great was ever achieved without enthusiasm."

   —Ralph Waldo Emerson

3. **Lighten Up Your Life with Humor:** "Humor" is a powerful motivator. The more humor and laughter in your life, the less stress you'll have, which means more positive energy to help you put your great attitude into action.

4. **Stay Motivated Through Exercise:** One of the best ways to move to a more positive and motivated frame of mind is to exercise. A regular exercise routine can provide relatively quick positive feedback in the form of weight loss, muscle development and a sense of doing something positive for yourself.

   [citation: Holman, Dr Ron. "December 2015 Attitude of Reflection." Association Los Angeles Deputy Sheriff's 1 Dec. 2015: 16-17. Print.]

Final Thoughts

Our Lord Jesus Christ describes to us the type of attitude that we should have, read: Matthew 6: 25-34. Christians have an attitude of gratitude. You could look at a glass as half empty or as half full. It is better to light a candle than curse the darkness.

The task ahead of you, is never as great as the power behind you. Be a messenger of hope.

When someone compliments you respond: "Whatever good I do comes from God and I thank Him for it."

When someone asks how I'm doing I respond: "I'm having a great day because JESUS loves me and I love HIM." Life is a song, love is the music and God is the composer. Spread Hope and Joy, if you are a Christian, you have a moral obligation to do so.

HOPE - Humility, Obedience, Prayer, Eucharist.

JOY – Jesus, Others, You.

Praising God in the Biblical Languages

Hebrew & Greek

Bevakasha (Hebrew) – Please

Bo (Hebrew) – Come; *Maranatha* (Greek) – Come

Lepo (Hebrew) – Here

Bevakasha bo "Abba" Hosanna – Please come Father save us

Bevakasha bo "Adonai" Hosanna – Please come Lord our Master save us

Bevakasha bo "Avinu Malkenu" Hosanna – Please come Our Father Our King save us

Bevakasha bo "El Elyon" Hosanna – Please come God the Most High save us

Bevakasha bo "Elohim" Hosanna – Please come All Powerful One - Creator save us

Bevakasha bo "El Shaddai" Hosanna – Please come God Almighty save us[74]

Bevakasha bo "Ezer"[75] *Hosanna* – Please come Helper save us

Bevakasha bo "Kurios"(Greek) *Hosanna* – Please come Lord save us

Bevakasha bo "Mefarnes"[76] *Hosanna* – Please come Provider save us

Bevakasha bo "Mekaddesh"[77] *Hosanna* – Please come Sanctifier save us

Bevakasha bo "Melchizedek"[78] *Hosanna* – Please come my King save us

Bevakasha bo "Rahv"[79] *Hosanna* – Please come Teacher save us

Bevakasha bo "Rohe"[80] *Hosanna* – Please come my Shepherd save us

Bevakasha bo "Rophe"[81] *Hosanna* – Please come Healer save us

Bevakasha bo "Ruach Qadesh"[82] *Hosanna* – Please come Holy Spirit save us

Bevakasha bo "Shammah"[83] *Hosanna* – Please come My Companion save us

Bevakasha bo "Theos"(Greek) *Hosanna* – Please come God save us

Bevakasha bo "Yeshua Moshiah" Hosanna – Please come Jesus Christ save us

Short Ejaculation Prayers

Amen (phonetically pronounced in Hebrew, 'Ah men') (CCC #2856) — So Be It

Ani Ohev Otkha – I Love you[84]

Ava rech otcha – Bless You[85]

Hagen Alino – Protect us, Defend us[86]

Hosanna – Save us

Jireh – will provide[87]

Kavod Tehilah Kavod[88] – Glory Praise Glory

L'haariytz (verb pronounced – leharitz)[89] – Worship

Tekadesh Otano – Sanctify Us[90]

Terahim otano – Have mercy on us[91]

Terahim oti – Have mercy on me[92]

Terapay – Heal us

Toda Rabah – Thank you very much

Yeshuah ho Elohim (Hebrew) – Jesus is God

Greek Doxology

Hagios o Theos (Greek) – Holy is God

Hagio Ischyros (Greek) – Holy and Mighty

Hagio Athanatos (Greek) – Holy and Immortal One

Eleison himas (Greek) – have mercy on us

Endnotes

1. Sheen, Fulton. "Prayer Is a Dialogue." *Your Life Is Worth Living – The Christian Philosophy of Life*. Schnecksville: St. Andrews, 2001. 337. Print.

2. "Chapter 3: The Life of Prayer." *Compendium, Catechism of the Catholic Church*. Washington, D.C.: United States Conference of Catholic Bishops, 2006. Print.

3. Ibid., 570.

4. *Magnificat*, Sept. 2014, Vol. 16, No 7, Peter John Cameron editor in chief, "What is Meditation", p.5.

5. Dr Vince Fortanasce – neurologist, treated St. John Paul II for Parkinson's. I Interviewed him on 9:30 a.m. Immaculate Heart radio 4-23-15; 12 noon to 1 p.m.

6. Ibid., 571.

7. Fr Peter John Cameron, O.P. Editor in Chief, *Magnificat* p.3, Editorial, July 2015, vol 17, no 5.

8. Porteus, Julian. *Manual of Minor Exorcisms: For the Use of Priests*. Catholic Truth Society, 0. Print.

9. This information on 'blessed salt' is taken from a pamphlet written by Fr. John Hampsch. You can obtain the pamphlet, tapes, and books by contacting his ministry at Claretian Tape Ministry, P.O. Box 19100, Los Angeles, CA 90019.

10. "Brown Scapular." *Scapular*. Web. 8 Dec. 2015. [http://carmelnet.org/scapular/scapular.htm].

11. "OSB. The Medal of Saint Benedict, Information, Description, History, Effects, and Suppliers." *OSB. The Medal of Saint Benedict, Information, Description, History, Effects, and Suppliers.*

Web. 8 Dec. 2015. [http://www.osb.org/gen/medal.html].

12. Fortea, Jose. "Chapter 5: Demonic Oppression and Possession." *Interview with an Exorcist: An Insider's Look at the Devil, Demonic Possession, and the Path to Deliverance.* West Chester, Penn.: Ascension, 2006. Print.

13. Fortea, Fr Antonio. "Curses, Spells, Evil Eye." *Curses, Spells, Evil Eye.* Web. 8 Dec. 2015.

14. Amorth, Father Gabriele. "Exorcisms and Prayer of Liberation." *An Exorcist–More Stories.* San Francisco: Ignatius, 2002. 94-95, 99. Print.

15. Euteneuer, Thomas J. "Chapter 2: The Devil, His Minions and His Activities." *Exorcism and the Church Militant.* Front Royal, Va.: Human Life International, 2010. p.46.

16. Jesus says: "I am the vine you are the branches apart from me you can do nothing…" (John 15:5)

17. Living in a State of Grace means to "live in friendship with God" and "walk humbly with God." Here are some examples…

    James 2:23 *"Abraham believed God, and it was reckoned to him as righteousness"; and he was called the friend of God."*

    James 4:4 *"Unfaithful creatures! Do you not know that friendship with the world is enmity with God? Therefore whoever wishes to be a friend of the world makes himself an enemy of God."*

    John 15:13-15 *"Greater love has no man than this, that a man lay down his life for his friends. You are my friends if you do what I command you. No longer do I call you servants, for the servant does not know what his master is doing; but I have called you friends…"*

    Micah 6:8 *"He has showed you, O man, what is good; and what does the LORD require of you but to do justice, and to love kindness, and to walk humbly with your God?*

18. Saunders, Father. "Why Go to Confession." *Ewtn.com*. "Arlington Catholic Herald.", 7 Apr. 1994. Web. 4 Dec. 2015.

19. Fortea, Jose. "Chapter 5: Demonic Oppression and Possession." *Interview with an Exorcist: An Insider's Look at the Devil, Demonic Possession, and the Path to Deliverance*. West Chester, Penn.: Ascension, 2006; p. 70 Print.

20. Amorth, Father Gabriele. "Exorcisms and Prayer of Liberation." *An Exorcist–More Stories*. San Francisco: Ignatius, 2002. p195. Print.

21. "The lives of many saints include examples of this affliction. Among modern saints, I can cite two who have been beatified by Pope John Paul II: Father Giovanni Calabria and Sister Mary of Jesus Crucified (who was the first Arab to be beatified). In both cases, and without any human fault, they were subjected to periods of true satanic possession. During those periods, the two saints did and said things totally incompatible with their holiness without the least fault, because it was the devil who acted through their bodies" (cf. An Exorcist tells His story, p. 57).

22. "Eucharistic Adoration." *Wikipedia*. Wikimedia Foundation, 14 Oct. 2015. Web. 4 Dec. 2015.

23. *Enchiridion Indulgentiarum*, 1968, Blessed Pope Paul VI.

24. Fr Peter John Cameron, O.P. "Meditation of the Day" - *Magnificat*; vol.15, no.6 / August 2013, p.70.

25. Fr Peter John Cameron, O.P. "Meditation of the Day" – *Magnificat*, vol.17, no.7 / Sept 2015, p.21.

26. Olmsted, Bishop Thomas. "Saints Our Heroes of Faith". *Into The Breach*. Phoenix: Knights of Columbus, 0. Print.

27. Debra Lipskys radio interview on 'demonic thought tampering' 4-23-13 (Tuesday); 11am to 12noon on Immaculate Heart Radio.

28. By the Envy of the Devil, Death Came in the World. *Catholic*

Encyclopedia, "Devil". N.p., n.d. Web. 28 Sept. 2016.

29. For example: *Playboy, Penthouse, Hustler,* Hollywood Movie Production companies, Pornography, Pimps and Prostitution, Terrorist organizations, Mexican Mafia cartels, Columbian Medellin cartels, the Italian Mafia, Motorcycle Outlaw Gangs, Planned Parenthood, the Democrat Party, University College Professors, the main stream Liberal Media etc.

30. Amorth, Gabriele. "Chapter 2: The Power of Satan." *An Exorcist Tells His Story*. San Francisco, Calif.: Ignatius, 1999. 29. Print.

31. Vianney, Fr John, "Chapter 5: On Temptations.", 8 Dec. 2015, [http://www.*Ewtn.com]*.

32. Contrite in latin means 'crushed' or 'ground to pieces.' "contrite". *Online Etymology Dictionary*. Douglas Harper, Historian. 07 Dec. 2015. Dictionary.com [http://dictionary.reference.com/browse/contrite].

33. Holy Name of Jesus (CCC #2668): The invocation of the holy name of Jesus is the simplest way of praying always. When the holy name is repeated often by a humbly attentive heart, the prayer is not lost by heaping up empty phrases, but holds fast to the word and "brings forth fruit with patience." This prayer is possible "at all times" because it is not one occupation among others but the only occupation: that of loving God, which animates and transfigures every action in Christ Jesus.

34. Spirutal Warfare Conference by Chad Ripperger F.S.S.P. (Feb. 19-21, 2012) at Holy Family Theater, Hollywood, CA. 1St Conference – "Ordinary Basics of Spiritual Warfare."

35. Apostolic Exhortation, 'Into the Breach' by Bishop Thomas Olmsted Diocese of Phoenix AZ, 9-29-15; p.1.

36. Lafave, Peter. "Battling the Demonic: An Interview with America's Exorcists; The Christian Review." *The Christian Review*. 2014. Web. 4 Dec. 2015.

37. The 'Foot of the Cross' is the *spiritual place* of our redemption which stands outside of time and space. Calvary is the place

where Satan was vanquished. There is a Latin phrase which explains this well: *Crux stat dum volvitur mundum* (The Cross remains still while the world revolves around it). In a similar vein, in the Eastern Catholic traditions, the "foot of the Cross" was code language for the *axis mundi* (the axis of the world) and was thought to be the center of the world, situated directly over hell. The priest symbolically stands at the foot of the Cross each day when he offers the Holy Sacrifice of the Mass. As exorcist, he calls down the precious blood of Jesus from the Cross to liberate the victim from the malevolent will of the demon. "The foot of the Cross" is that place where all humans may spiritually retreat to receive refreshment and grace; it is the ultimate Tribunal where Christ judges all demons because it was the place where Satan himself was judged (taken from: 'Exorcism and the Church Militant' by Reverend Thomas Euteneuer, p.184).

38. Cameron, John, Fr, ed. "Jubilee Year of Mercy." *Magnificat* July 2016: 5. Print.

39. The Holy Bible on 'free will'. Sirach 15:11-17, 20: "Do not say, "Because of the Lord I left the right way"; for he will not do what he hates. Do not say, "It was he who led me astray"; for he has no need of a sinful man. The Lord hates all abominations, and they are not loved by those who fear him. It was he who created man in the beginning, and he left him in the power of his own inclination. If you will, you can keep the commandments, and to act faithfully is a matter of your own choice. He has placed before you fire and water: stretch out your hand for whichever you wish. Before a man are life and death, and whichever he chooses will be given to him…He has not commanded anyone to be ungodly, and he has not given anyone permission to sin."

40. Holman, Dr Ron. "Coping Skils to Deal Wit Daily Stress." *The ALADS Dispatcher* 1 Aug. 2014, Summer 2014 ed., Managed Behavorial Health Care Services sec.: 16-17. Print.

41. Ibid.

42. Ibid.

43. Ibid.

44. Ibid.

45. Dr. Taylor Marshall, "The Difference Between Dark Night of the Soul and Dark Night of the Senses (According to St. John of the Cross)", N.p. 2012. Web 26 Sept. 2016, [http://taylormarshall.com/2012/09/the-difference-between-dark-night-of.html].

46. Dr Mark Miravelle, "Christian Spirituality", online course, 18 July 2002, Franciscan University of Steubenville, Ohio, Classroom Lecture.

47. Emily Stimpson, *OSV Newsweekly*, contributing editor, "Understanding the Dark Night of the Soul", 20 May 2015, [https://www.osv.com/OSVNewsweekly/ByIssue/Article/TabId/735/ArtMID/13636/ArticleID/17512/Understanding-the-%e2%80%98dark-night-of-the-soul%e2%80%99-.aspx].

48. Glenn, N.D. and Weaver, C.N., "A Multivariate, Multi-Survey Study of Marital Happiness," *Journal of Marriage and the Family*, 40 (1978): 269-282] and [Schumm, W.R., Bollman, S.R., and Jurich, A.P., "The 'Marital Conventionalization' Argument Implications for the Study of Religiosity and Marital Satisfaction," *Journal of Psychology and Theology*, 10, no. 3 (1982): 236-241.

49. National Institute of Healthcare Research of America; Dr Michael McCullough, June 2000, [http://www.psy.miami.edu/faculty/mmccullough/Papers/rel_mort_meta.pdf].

50. William T. Martin, "Religiosity and United States Suicide Rates, 1972-1978," *Journal of Clinical Psychology*, Vol. 40 (1984), pp. 1166-1169 and Steven Stack, "The Effect of Domestic-Religious Individualism on Suicide", 1954-1978, "*Journal of Marriage and the Family"*, Vol. 47 (1985), pp. 431-447.

51. *Journal of Gerontology*: Medical Sciences on a study conducted in N. Carolina by Duke. [http://www.dukespiritualityandhealth.org/pastreports.html#attendance].

52. Dr. Harold Koenig, a researcher at Duke University Medical Center, [http://www.vibrantlife.com/?p=218].

53. Dr. Jeff Levin, a social epidemiologist and medical school professor, University of North Carolina in Chapel Hill, [http://www.vibrantlife.com/?p=218].

54. *Faith & Family: The Core Strengths of American Society* by Patrick F. Fagan, William G. FitzGerald Fellow in Family and Cultural Issues, The Heritage Foundation, Washington D.C.

55. Dr. Harold Koenig, a researcher at Duke University Medical Center, [http://www.vibrantlife.com/?p=218].

56. *Faith & Family: The Core Strengths of American Society* by Patrick F. Fagan, William G. FitzGerald Fellow in Family and Cultural Issues, the Heritage Foundation, Washington D.C.

57. Day, J.M. and Laufer, W.S., editors *Crime, Values and Religion* (Ablex Publishing Corporation: Norwood, NJ: 1987) 113 as cited by Maginnis, R.L., *Religion and Crime: Age-Old Enemies,* Insight for Family Research Council.

58. According to research by Dr David Larson from the National Institute for Health Care Research (NIHR), [http://www.vibrantlife.com/?p=218].

59. Larson, D.B. and Wilson, W.P., "Religious Life of Alcoholics," *Southern Medical Journal*, 73, no. 6 (1980): 723-727.

60. Barbara R. Lorch and Robert H. Hughes, "Religion and Youth Substance Use," *Journal of Religion and Health,* Vol. 24 (1985), pp. 197-208.

61. *Why Religion Matters: The Impact of Religious Practice on Social Stability* by Patrick Fagan, Ph.D., January 25, 1996. Freeman, R.R., "Who Escapes? The Relation of Church-going and Other Background Factors to the Socioeconomic Performance of Black Male Youths from Inner-city Poverty Tracks," working paper no. 1656, National Bureau of Economic Research, Cambridge, MA, (June 1985) as cited by VanDenBerghe, E., "Religion and the Abundant Life," *Church of Jesus Christ Official Magazine-*

Enzyme/Endtime.

62. Myers, D. G. (2000). On assessing prayer, faith, and health. *Reformed Review*, 53(2), 119–126, [http://www.davidmyers.org/religion/faith.html].

63. Thornton, A. and Camburn, D., "Religious Participation and Adolescent Sexual Behavior and Attitudes," *Journal of Marriage and the Family*, 51 (Aug. 1989): 641-653.

64. David Larson's - "Sex in America" study published in 1995, and conducted by sociologists from the University of Chicago and the State University of New York at Stonybrook, also showed very high sexual satisfaction among "conservative" religious women with their husbands than do moderately religious or non-religious women http://www.heritage.org/research/reports/1996/01/bg1064nbsp-why-religion-matters.

65. Christopher F. Scott and Susan Sprecher, "Sexuality in Marriage, Dating, and Other Relationships: A Decade Review," *Journal of Marriage and Family*, Vol. 62, No. 4 (November 2000), pp. 999–1017.

66. Research psychiatrists at the Duke University Department of Psychiatry concluded this in 1992 http://www.heritage.org/research/reports/1996/01/bg1064nbsp-why-religion-matters#108.

67. Sixty years of research - 1930 to 1990). Jenkins, K., "Religion and Families" in Bahr, S.J., *Family Research: A Sixty Year Review*, 1930-1990, 2 vols. (New York: Macmillan, 1991) 1:235-288.

68. Alar, S., "An Experimental Study of the Effects of Distant, Intercessory Prayer on Self-Esteem, Anxiety, and Depression," *Alternative Therapies in Health and Medicine* 3 (6), (1997): 38-53.

69. Dr. Harold Koenig, a researcher at Duke University Medical Center; http://www.dukehealth.org/health_library/news/491.

70. Stephanie A. Bond Huie, Robert A. Hummer, and Richard G. Rogers,"Individual and Contextual Risks of Death among Race and Ethnic Groups in the United States," *Journal of Health*

and Social Behavior,Vol. 43 (2002), pp. 359–381.

71. In 1988 Dr. Randolph Byrd conducted a study pertaining to patients that came in having heart attacks or severe chest pains. Dr. Byrd is a cardiologist at San Francisco General Hospital, His study was entitled "Positive Therapeutic Effects of Intercessory Prayer in a Coronary Care Unit Population" and was in the *Southern Medical Journal* and then was republished again in 1997 by *Alternative Therapies*, Vol. 3, No. 6. Dr. Byrd randomly appointed approximately 400 patients in the coronary-care unit to either a grouping that received daily prayers or a grouping that did not. When they were discharged, the study found that those that had been prayed for were much less likely to need antibiotics or develop complications. [http://www.angelfire.com/realm/soulseeking0/healings.html].

72. An article published by the Hartford Institute for Religion Research, based on studies by J. Bartowski, B.Wilcox and C. Ellison. Bartowski, J.P., W.B. Wilcox, and C.G. Ellison, "Parenting and Evangelical Families," Hartford Institute for Religion Research (2001).

73. *Legacy* by Steve Wood p.127 taken from "Thomas Karras, "The Truth about Men and the Church" reporting on a 1994 Swiss Study in Vol.2 of *Population Studies* no 31.

74. Corrected by Dr Andrew Swafford; professor of biblical theology and Languages at Benedictine College, Atchinson Kansas; aswafford@benedictine.edu.

75. Ibid.

76. Ibid., – 'provider' [noun] – m'far'nes (pronounced) –mefarnes.

77. Ibid.

78. Melchizedek means – 'My King' – [http://www.hebrew4christians.com/Scripture/Parashah/Summaries/Lekh_Lekha/Melchizedek/melchizedek.html].

79. [http://www.answers.com/Q/What_does_rabbi_mean_in_Hebrew/].

80. Corrected by Dr Andrew Swafford; professor of biblical theology and Languages at Benedictine College, Atchinson Kansas; aswafford@benedictine.edu.

81. Ibid.

82. Ibid.

83. "Names of God from the Old Testament" (Wall Chart); 2005 Research Inc. Rose Publishing Inc., 4733 Torrance Blvd., #259, Torrance CA 90503. www.rose-publishing.com.

84. Translated by Amer Shehadeh – Authorized Holy Land Guide: fluent English, Hebrew, Arabic – BestouR Tours. He is an Israeli Palestinian Catholic Christian.

85. Verified: [http://www.doitinhebrew.com].

86. Translated by Amer Shehadeh.

87. Corrected by Dr Andrew Swafford; professor of biblical theology and Languages at Benedictine College, Atchinson Kansas; aswafford@benedictine.edu.

88. Corrected by Dr Andrew Swafford; professor of biblical theology and Languages at Benedictine College, Atchinson Kansas; aswafford@benedictine.edu.

89. Translated by Amer Shehadeh.

90. Ibid.

91. Ibid.

92. "Names of God from the Old Testament" (Wall Chart); 2005 Research Inc. Rose Publishing Inc., 4733 Torrance Blvd., #259, Torrance CA 90503. www.rose-publishing.com.